Praise for
A Portrait of the Piss Artist as a Young Man

'Tadhg has mastered the skill of making the difficult shit that us humans deal with in life accessible, through a beautiful irreverent cocktail of vulnerability, hilarity, emotional intelligence and charm'
— **Niall Breslin, aka Bressie**

'An amazing story of addiction and redemption'
— **Paul Howard, author of the Ross O'Carroll-Kelly series**

'Hickey's memoir is self-deprecating and well-paced, but the liveliness is a smokescreen for his more serious intent. However familiar the addiction arc, Hickey's candour could actually really help people, especially those noticing the "craic" mutating into something decidedly less fun'
— *Irish Times*

'[A] memoir of catastrophe and eventual triumph'
— *Independent Westmeath*

'You'd be forgiven for thinking a silly book awaits, but, though there are some chuckles and Hickey writes with an amiable levity throughout, what you actually get is an impressively clear-eyed account of alcoholism, which Hickey likens to "having a twin brother who hates you",'
— **Rory Kiberd,** *Irish Times*

'Tadhg Hickey has really put his heart and soul into this memoir of catastrophe and eventual triumph, and I hope it sells and sells. If nothing else, it's an inspiration to anyone who may be having similar problems'
— **Anne Cunningham,** *The Connaught Telegraph*

'Humorous, touching and redemptive'
— *Irish Examiner*

Tadhg Hickey is a comedian, actor, writer, director, voice-over artist and an alcoholic. He has written and performed sitcoms and Player series for RTÉ, his viral sketches have achieved global critical and media acclaim, and his one-man shows enjoy sell-out tours throughout Ireland and the UK. He lives in the best city in the best country in the world – Cork, Ireland, obviously – with his partner and child. The piss artist's newborn needs nappies, so buy this book.

A Portrait of the Piss Artist as a Young Man

Tadhg Hickey

eriu

First published by Eriu
An imprint of Black & White Publishing Group
A Bonnier Books UK company

4th Floor, Victoria House,
Bloomsbury Square,
London, WC1B 4DA

Owned by Bonnier Books
Sveavägen 56, Stockholm, Sweden

Twitter – @eriu_books
Instagram – @eriubooks

Hardback – 978-1-80418-359-5
Trade Paperback – 978-1-80418-381-6
Paperback – 9781-80418-343-4
Ebook – 978-1-80418-382-3

All rights reserved. No part of the publication may be reproduced, stored in
a retrieval system, transmitted or circulated in any form or by any means,
electronic, mechanical, photocopying, recording or otherwise, without prior
permission in writing of the publisher.

A CIP catalogue of this book is available from the British Library.

Designed by Graham Thew
Printed and bound by Clays Ltd., Elcograf S.p.A

1 3 5 7 9 10 8 6 4 2

Copyright © Tadhg Hickey 2024

Tadhg Hickey has asserted their moral right to be identified as the author of this
Work in accordance with the Copyright, Designs and Patents Act 1988.

Every reasonable effort has been made to trace copyright holders of material
reproduced in this book, but if any have been inadvertently overlooked the
publishers would be glad to hear from them.

Eriu is an imprint of Bonnier Books UK
www.bonnierbooks.co.uk

To Mam, the cure and the cause

Preface

When I was a kid in primary school, I took some newspaper from a stack in the classroom and laid it on my table to protect it during painting. The page I had unknowingly selected turned out to be a Page Three of a glamour model from a tabloid. When they saw the content, the other kids gathered around excitedly. My teacher approached my desk and looked at me as if I was a dirty little boy who had sought out the image and satiated myself with it before sharing the sleazy spoils with my fellow sex pests.

Maybe I *was* a dirty little boy because, even though I didn't choose the page deliberately, I had enjoyed looking at the woman. That night, while I slept, the woman came to visit me in my dreams. She stood at the end of my bed, dressed seductively. I hardly recognised her with her clothes on. She encouraged me out of the bed and towards her but, as I did so, her mouth opened and a cluster of snakes rushed towards me and pinned me back onto the bed. I woke up screaming.

The dream epitomised my thinking when I was a child: that there was a good path, that probably wasn't all that much fun, but it was the path that I 'should' be on. This path was flanked by neighbours and teachers patting me on the back and telling me I was a 'good boy'.

1

Then there was the bad path. That path would bring transitory pleasure but the trade-off was ungodly pain and suffering. The good ol' Catholic upbringing, ha? It's hard to beat it for terror. God is good, evil is bad, they are both inside you and you must show the moral strength and courage to ensure God wins out. This thinking accompanied me all the way through my drinking, which began on exams night 1998 and ended (up to the time of writing) with me drinking alone on the street in London in 2015.

To imagine that there was an evil force operating my alcoholism from within, steering me towards torture and death, created two interrelated concerns for me: 1. If the devil is inside me, I would think, actively ruining my life, doesn't that take away a lot of personal accountability? 2. It was fucking terrifying. I spent years frazzled and fearful of this devil-inside idea, which seems a bit of a waste of time for a hunch.

I don't have any hard evidence to support the idea that I was walking around Cork with a demon at my controls. What I do know for sure, and what these cognitive cul-de-sacs I went down seem to prove, is that my thinking was deranged. It was my balm-pot (Corkish for 'mad') thinking that started in childhood and festered unchecked right up until the endgame with the ol' drinking that was my problem. And while I couldn't do much about the devil, there was a lot I could do about my thinking problem.

But what the hell am I talking about, says you? 'Anxiety, mental illness, thinking problems? I thought you were an alcoholic, Hickey – what's all this mental-health rubbish got to do with drinking your bodyweight in whiskey?' This, in a nutshell, is why I wrote this book. I reckon we in Ireland know all about alcohol but little or nothing about alcoholism. Alcoholism is a mental illness, guys. That's not my theory, it's the World Health Organization's position. No one goes AWOL on drinking sprees for days or weeks, ruins their own life and the lives of their loved ones, and pursues drinking, some all the way to the grave, because they're simply selfish or stupid. They're mentally unwell (or at least, I've come to believe I was and still can be if I'm not doing the right things). That's not a cop out. Selfishness is a factor but most of us are drinking our heads off to treat our mental illness and ease the pain of the trauma we carry. We're using alcohol to cope with our alcoholism. Steve-O from *Jackass*, a recovering alcoholic, once said that his alcoholism only really began when he stopped drinking. The drinking is not the beginning and end of the illness, it's just a symptom.

But this is not a self-help book. I have no idea what will work for you if you find yourself trapped, lost or struggling – I only know what worked for me. It's not a drinkalogue, although there are many chaotic and funny drinking stories. This is a book about a mental illness called alcoholism. My alcoholism, because I'm only speaking for myself. It's a book about developing the illness, treating it with alcohol, hitting a series of rock bottoms and finally finding a way into recovery.

Real recovery, not simply stopping drinking – as all that effectively did was take away my anaesthetic. I mean a mountable route up out of the madness.

And if there's hope in these pages it's that at various times in my life, I thought I was a dead man. I felt like a character in a video game on his last life with the power bar almost at zero. If I didn't drink myself to death, I was liable to think myself there. But I'm not dead. And I'm in good ol' form. And these days, if I have a dream about a snake-breathing seductress, I don't mistake it for a biblical condemnation of my moral character, that I am some class of a sleazy St Patrick, who must banish the snakes from the glamour-model industry to save his soul, I just try to enjoy it.

Chapter One

The Hickey Bunch

The Lord above, he is my usher
He is my vision 'cause I don't see.
My tears, my trials, my tribulations
He doth erase them from the scene.

In one eye and out the other, they do flow
And the Lord, our God, collects them as he goes.

When I was a boy, I was world weary
Before He taught me how not to see
Happy with my lot, I'm now impervious
To those who are scurrilous. I am free.

In one eye and out the other, they do flow
And the Lord, our God, collects them as he goes.
And the Lord, our God, collecting all our woes.

From the play *In One Eye, Out the Other* by
Tadhg Hickey

It's 2022 and I approach the Everyman Theatre feeling
pure *sceitimíní áthas* (excitedly happy) in the tummy. I've
had a bit of a buckaroo of a year to say the least but it

feels like things are finally falling into place. My partner and I have had good news: it's Christmas and the gig I'm about to do promises to be a right dote of a thing. I'm MC-ing a community concert featuring talent from war-ravaged Ukraine as well as mixed-race Irish rappers and DJs. I'm just starting to feel smug about how early I am for the sound check when I'm told I'm late: a microcosm for my life.

I hit the stage and before we launch into a company rehearsal of 'Jingle Bells', I take in the splendour of the Everyman one more time. I've been lucky enough to perform on many big Irish stages but they're all muck compared to Cork's Victorian jewel. (NB I'd like to distance myself from that 'muck' comment straight away. I only put it in to suck up to the Everyman but I'm eager to be seen to be sucking up to promoters of all big venues everywhere. I digress.) Maybe it's because I'm a Cork City boy but there is something uniquely charming about the Everyman for me: the ubiquitous red (Santa-suit Christmas red), the elaborate proscenium arch, but with decorated boxes that look like they were made and inserted last minute. It's this mix of kitsch and cool that makes the Everyman, and indeed Cork, so heartbreakingly perfect.

I'm surprisingly hit and miss with 'Jingle Bells'. My head is elsewhere. I've been doing the psychotherapy thing and have been struggling with going back into childhood and feeling the feelings, as they say. I'm trying to get my head around the concept of the 'inner child'. The idea of the little guy or gal inside who because he or she didn't get what they needed as a smallie, still gets scared and sad and causes manifold troubles for the adult might be clichéd old hat to you but I've never been in therapy before. Where I grew up in Cork, therapy meant get drunk, go to Mass or a mixture of the two. Therapy seemed like something middle-class people from Rochestown or Crosshaven might do; you'd picture them banging on about their inner children in the Marks & Spencer's café or something. But now I wish I had been one of them because I'm out of my depth. My therapist has suggested 'developing a relationship with him', doing something with him that he'd enjoy. I'd imagine a decent percentage of Cork already thinks I'm off my game. If I'm seen running around Patrick Street laughing and joking with an invisible infant, I'm done.

The rehearsal is over and I'm not embarrassed to say I'm on the YouTube cramming the 'Jingle Bells' harmony. Confident, and with a while to go before the gig, I close my eyes and I try to picture the ol' inner child to see what he's up to.

I am the youngest of five children, a 'surprise' who arrived a full ten years after my nearest sibling. I grew up in McCurtain villas on the southside of Cork City. McCurtain villas was, at least from my weird class-obsessed perspective, torn between two very different lovers. On one side was College Road and Mardyke Walk with its resplendent Victorian houses, the fee paying Presentation Boys College (secondary school), the Cork County Cricket club and Sunday's Well Tennis Club. That lover had clearly done alright for himself but he was a bit dull. On the other side was Barrack Street. He hadn't a pot to piss in or a window to throw it out of but boy was he exciting. Barrack Street's a bit bougie these days, but when I was a nipper it was the Wild West with more pubs than sense. Barrack Street was probably a bit too hard for me, the Cricket Club brigade were too soft, so McCurtain villas was just right!

Let me introduce the Hickey Bunch. Pops was a tough-but-terrific hardworking lad from Mayfield. I don't know why I'm calling him a lad because from as early as I can remember, I thought of him as an old man, or at least much older than my friends' dads. He was whispering at 50 when I was born and from the get-go I worried he was going to die. He had no major health issues but I just worried. Then there was Mam. (We called her 'Mam' generally, 'Mumsie' ironically. 'Mum' = Rochestown; 'Mom' = cop on to yourself). She really deserves a book in herself. Although she enjoyed playing the patsy, she was razor sharp. Even when I had long grown up, she'd sometimes ring me up and ask me to call to the house because she couldn't find a particular TV channel she liked (probably that American one that shows Mass on a loop) or she'd accidentally put teletext on and couldn't get it off again. You might be thinking, *Sure, God love the poor woman*, but it was more often than not chican-ery designed to tether you to her. If you didn't take the bait, she'd magically be able to find channels and restore

TV order with no help from anyone. In spite of her many issues, which I'll get to, she ruled the roost and deployed whatever tactics necessary to do so.

When I was a kid, my eldest bro Declan, 17 years my senior, was a flamboyant and startlingly handsome wild child of a big brother, but I don't remember doing too much with him because he was already married and had moved out by the time I knew what was going on. I do have one recollection of probably being about four or five and him swinging me round and round the garden by the hands, my legs flailing in the wind, my mam hysterically demanding he put me down, and me screaming, 'Deccy, Deccy, Deccy!' partly scared, partly absolutely exhilarated. Thinking about it now, it's a perfectly Hickey moment somehow. My brother Alan is of a similar age to Dec but didn't get married or move out as young, so we'd much more time to bond. He is very similar to my dad: soft, playful and warm when you're on his good side, but ferocious if you're ever stupid enough to wander over to the other. Like Dec, he is a man's man, hard-working, good with his hands and practical. I was the opposite of all these things and yet we always had an understanding and a strong connection. As I was so much younger than my two eldest brothers I didn't really have that brotherly rivalry with them. At various stages they both treated me as if I could be their kid. They'd take the piss out of me for being Mam's favourite boy but there was no malice to it. Besides, I *was* Mam's favourite.

Next came my brother Con who, because of severe physical and intellectual disabilities, lived most of his life in The Cope Foundation, a beautiful, miraculous Cork institution, which has been a lifesaver for people with intellectual and physical challenges and their families. I used to visit him regularly and we had a good ol' bond. When my head used to be deranged in later life, I'd go to Glasheen and sit with him in his room and gratefully accept the peace that time with him would gift you. He was non-verbal but he'd shout or laugh or pull your hair if he wanted your undivided attention. I wouldn't have used the word at the time but it was probably with Con that I had my first experiences of spirituality. He seemed pure to me, uninhibited by the obsession with being noticed or validated that I and most people in my life seemed to be caught up in.

My sister Deborah is closest in age to me and there's no one on this planet who influenced my young mind more than her. She was the reason I wrote the lyrics to Doors' songs on my primary school copybooks. The Doors, Pink Floyd, Led Zeppelin, The Police – all were discovered in her LP collection. She also fostered, even co-created, my sense of humour. I was definitely still in primary school when I would regularly watch shows like *The Young Ones* on RTÉ on a Friday night, doing the voices, acting out the scenes. I worshipped the sister and although she can't possibly have been happy about it, everywhere she went, I followed. I loved hanging out with her friends, who became one of my first audiences. One of my happiest childhood memories is of Deb taking me by the hand into her school, Saint Aloysius, to watch *Santa Claus the Movie* with her and her classmates. How or why I was there, I couldn't tell you. But the experience was pure magic. Not just the movie itself, but the dimming of the lights, the anticipation of the projector turning on, not to mention the excitement and intrigue of going behind the walls of a school for GIRLS! They seemed so mysterious to me and smelled way better than lads. They were really cool, and none more so than my sister.

We were a pretty typical working-class Cork family, I reckon. Well, actually, before I came along, they were probably knocking on the middle-class door. My dad had a great job in Ford's car manufacturers, which was then the biggest employer in the city. We'd get a swanky new Cortina every year which was the envy of the neighbours. We weren't a foreign-holiday type of family but the pre-Tadhg Hickeys were seemingly fairly comfortable. I don't remember these dizzy heights at all because when I was still a baby, Ford's closed forever. That wasn't supposed to happen. As Conal Creedon put it beautifully in his play *The Cure*, it was supposed to be 'a job for life'.

It was 1980s Ireland and my father, though industrious, found it hard to find or create work that would bring in anything like the money he made in Ford's. He was already in his fifties and it was the beginning of one of the most brutal recessions in the history of the State but he was relentless in his pursuit of work. He sold soft drinks out of a car, went door to door with the football pools (the forerunner of the Lotto), provided optics to pubs – he was always on the go, always trying, but in spite of his best efforts, the good times never returned. The family's fortunes started to tank just as I came along, which was rude. I was like the guy who arrives at the party on day three and all the cans are gone and everyone's coming down.

For the first few years of my life there were four of us kids at home as well as Mam and Dad, Con having already transitioned to residential care in Cope. I was acutely aware there wasn't money to spare. Now, I was no Oliver Twist. I might get a bike or even a Commodore 64 games console for Christmas but they were second hand. I went to school and onto college with the help of grants and welfare support. I never did things outside school, like swimming or drama, because I knew we hadn't the money. The ride to school was in a beat-up Toyota Corolla rather than the pristine new Cortina from Ford's. In later years, when I started becoming obsessed with James Joyce and read that his family had gotten increasingly poorer as his childhood progressed, I took it as a deep and undeniable sign that I either was him or I was destined for similar greatness.

To a lot of my friends, though, I was actually posh. I lived in a house but a lot of the lads I hung out with lived in flats. Yet in my fairly middle-class school in Bishopstown I felt self-conscious that I didn't have the right clothes or football gear. Class seems to depend on your perspective. But that is not to say that class doesn't exist as I've heard others posit. I fell off my chair reading the following sentence in a recent RTÉ review of a Damien Dempsey show: 'And anyway, the idea of class is a load of nonsense, really.' Is it? Tell that to the guy or girl who, though qualified, doesn't get the job because they don't have the right look or accent. Class is only a load of nonsense if it doesn't affect you. At the same time, I must constantly be on the watch for my proclivity to lean on the working-class identity too much. We didn't have much but we were alright, like; I never slept on the street or went hungry. I probably looked on other families with envy. Some of the lads in the flats probably looked at us with envy. And vast swathes of the Global South enduring the brutal effects of neocolonialism would no doubt look at what we in the West describe as poverty and scratch their heads.

I have two particularly clear early memories. (Or, at least, two I like to think about.) I don't know which one came first but they both involve my dad. Pops was an ordinary working-class Cork man in many ways but to me he was extraordinary. He just seemed to be naturally really good at being a citizen of the world. He'd do things for people without any fuss or fanfare, which, even as a kid, was confusing to me. My philosophy then – and sometimes even now – can be, 'What's the point in doing something for someone if it's not on the front page of the *Echo*?' (The following isn't one of the two memories, I'll come back to them in a minute. You might as well settle in for tangents like this.)

Mrs S. was a neighbour of ours and she was almost cartoonish in her meanness. If you accidentally kicked your plastic cup champions football into her garden, she was wont to emerge out her front door with a bread knife, plunge it into the poor ball and hold it aloft like a merciless warrior brazenly ridiculing you with your own severed head. So why was this dangerous psychopath standing at my front door? That she was smiling and appeared to be holding a freshly baked apple tart was yet more unnerving. It transpired that the apple tart was a token of appreciation for my father who had been doing odd jobs for her around her house over several months. This floored me. What kind of a person keeps something like that to themselves? You'd been helping out an old lady, a wretched one at that, and you didn't seek kudos? What kind of a sick mind are we dealing with here? But, more to the point, it confirmed my view that Pops was naturally adept at being a good person.

Anyway, back to the memories, says you. In the first, I must be about five years old. I'm standing on Cork's famous Shandon Street. It was a baking hot summer's day and my eyes were bouncing between a delicious 99 ice cream, which was dripping chaotically over my fat little hand, and my dad, who was stood looking out over the city, demolishing his own 99 without so much as an errant drip. He looked like an aquiline gladiator. Always stood upright, no slouching. He was from the same neck of the woods in Cork as Roy Keane, who also has that 'don't come fucking near me' posture. Must be a Mayfield thing. Mine was a busy house and it wasn't often you'd get Dad on his own, but my mother was off shopping in the Dunnes Stores on North Main Street so I had him all to myself. I was just stood there, looking at my dad looking at Cork. I assumed he owned the place. He was bald and proud, playful and formidable, and he was *my* dad. I was very happy to be knocking around with him.

The second memory is more portentous. I was in a sadly departed bar called Maudy Whelan's on North Main Street with Dad. Although I was probably only six or seven, I was somehow competing in a pool tournament with a bunch of grown men. Dinner was a packet of King crisps and a bottle of Lucozade and I was having the time of my life. (To this day, I'm a swashbuckling pool player. In fact, it's a really easy tell if you're trying to figure out if someone's from a working-class, drink-sodden background: they're almost invariably pool sharks because they grew up in pubs.) But the key component of that memory is not so much the pool, or the crisps, or the Lucozade, or even my dad. It's drink. I wasn't actually drinking, of course, but the spectacle, the smell, the consequential merriness of other people were captivating to me: men singing songs in the pisser, the ball-hoppin' (Corkish for mocking), the tall tales, the transformation of mood. These lads had shuffled in a couple of hours ago shaky and shy – two or three pints later they were composites of Luke Kelly and Dave Allen. What was this strange tarry elixir breathing life into all these lost souls? I was intoxicated by the pub long before I ever drank.

One event confirmed my belief that my dad was a super-hero. Genuinely, like. I was sitting on the sofa in the living room watching *Unsolved Mysteries* on the TV instead of doing my homework. The next thing I knew, the kitchen seemed to explode. There was a cacophonous blast and then a fireball scorched through the kitchen furniture. What we didn't realise then but found out later was that the oil fire had malfunctioned and burst into flames. In rapid, assured movements, my father ushered me, my mother and my brother (who had been upstairs sick in bed) out the front door to safety. Then he proceeded to the kitchen to tackle the oil fire. When he attempted to pick it up, it exploded again in his face causing severe burns to his head and body. As we stood on the road doing nothing but watch the smoke and flames in the kitchen and worry, my father was burning and fighting for his life. And yet, with the kitchen entirely ablaze, he somehow managed to lift the oil fire again on his own and break the kitchen window with it. From there, he threw it and himself out through the window and onto the ground and broken glass, not only saving himself and his whole family but also our house, and all before the fire brigade even got there.

I was in fifth class at the time and we had to do an assignment about our hero. I'm gonna be honest here and say I had intended to write about Paul McGrath.

That performance in Giants Stadium against the Italians in 1994 is something that, even today, I think about regularly. But Paul never risked his life for me. I changed my hero to my dad. I wrote that even though he was a Norrie (Cork Northsider) I didn't hold it against him and I really loved him and he was the bravest dad I knew. I couldn't wait for him to come out of the hospital, where he was receiving treatment for his burns, and be home again. I had tried not to show it but the first night I visited him in hospital I was shocked by how he looked – his head in particular was terrifying to me. It was at least twice its natural size and I remember his skin looking like orange rubber. But I was also in awe. Breaking windows and fighting fires? That was Superman stuff. I thought he was going to die in the fire but he didn't. Maybe he wasn't ever going to die. He was a superhero after all.

Seemingly without even trying, Dad was showing me how to navigate the world like he did. A tough-guy hero, but mild-mannered and charming when he wanted to be. My dad was just himself. He didn't feel the need to hog the limelight or to be somebody he wasn't in order to be liked or accepted – something I became very good at and have spent a lifetime trying to undo. One evening, I was playing pool with him in a pub called Ellis's on Gillabbey Street. My dad looked a bit like Sean Connery – and not just because both of them were bald – and these American tourists were excitedly chatting to him, earnestly believing him to be the famous actor. He dealt with it in such a relaxed and generous way, neither taking the piss with a silly accent nor crushing their illusion maliciously. I seem to remember him telling them he was Sean's first cousin. I was envious of my dad's momentary star status. I was about eight or nine at the time and was very eager to get in on the action. I put on the charm offensive and started whipping the cue out of his hand before he'd even taken his shots. I was doing tricks and commentating on my brilliance. I was half mad with the longing for attention and got my few laughs from the tourists. But after they'd gone on their way, my dad gently pulled me aside and said, 'I know you were only having a laugh, but there's no need to be rude when you're doing it.' Wow. Have you ever been at a party where somebody entertaining is telling a story, and some painful attention-seeking klutz wrecks it with charmless interjections? It's probably unusual for an eight-year-old to find a rebuke from a parent to be balanced and fair, but that's how I felt. I admired the way he let me have my little moment and didn't embarrass me in front of my captive audience.

But Pops wasn't perfect. My editor, my psychotherapist and countless friends over the years have pointed out my tendency to put my father on a pedestal. I think all of his kids do it. I mean, I have literally just spent the last few pages selling you his superhero credentials. It's a brand new concept for me to even consider imperfections in his parenting. But I suppose I've learned the hard way that blaming my mother for everything and making her the devil is unhelpful. So, making Dad God is probably equally futile.

In one of the last sessions I had with my therapist, I was describing in some detail a particularly horrific experience I had with my mother. This is my specialised subject, so I was really giving it all that. My therapist (Bubbsie – I have a tendency to nickname people, particularly those who are important in my life) interrupted my tale of woe and asked one fairly straightforward question: 'Where was your dad when all this was going on?' I couldn't answer her. When I was at the coalface of my mother's madness, my dad was generally absent from the scene.

Dad also had a fiery temper. My eldest brother Declan, by his own admission, was what we euphemistically call in Cork, a 'wilder' who got into trouble with the law, and, like myself, had a chaotic relationship with alcohol. My dad's best efforts to get him to toe the line would sometimes amount to just beating the shit out of him. These beatings were before my time and of a time, and moralising about them is pointless, but one thing is certain: they were ineffective. They were counterproductive in helping my brother with whatever was going on for him to make him act out. He understandably just got wilder.

By the time yours truly burst onto the scene, my dad had chilled out considerably. But I still had that healthy fear of the man. I was very much aware that he had the potential to explode and you didn't wanna be the reason the bomb went off. I remember my brothers often marvelling at the way I would speak to him. I was just that little bit cheekier with Pops than they would've ever dared to be but I didn't always know the line. I remember asking to borrow a pair of his socks one time and playfully working my way through the options criticising each pair as I went, tossing them aside disappointedly: 'Rubbish, brutal, old-fashioned' etc. I thought I was in the middle of a tidy little comedy routine but I had misjudged the mood of my audience completely. Unexpectedly, he jumped up out of his chair, scooped all the socks up in one movement and said something like, 'I'll take them away so if they're not good enough for you.' His face was contorted and his eyes were mad and I was fucking terrified. If he was a father today, he might have watched an Instagram reel on parenting and promptly apologised to me for his inability to 'process his feelings', for transferring his fears and frustrations onto me, and offered to buy me an assortment of funky socks to win back my love and trust. But this was early-nineties Ireland, so I just stayed out of his way until he cooled down and then we did what all Irish families did at the time: swept the unnerving incident, along with all the others, under the carpet.

My fascination and veneration of the father extended all the way to drink and how to do it. When he was boozed up in the pub his eyes would go a little glassy and he'd be more likely to smoke a Major and sing a romantic ballad like 'Sweet Sixteen' to my mam. He had a sweet singing voice, actually, and even as young as I was, I could see that drink mostly had a positive effect on him. None of us know exactly what is going on behind someone else's forehead but from where I was looking, he had it all figured out. After a few pints he'd be merry, in the thick of the sing-song, but the vast majority of the time he'd leave it at that and be up early in the morning working or looking after his family. It was kind of an unspoken principle in my house and community that if you couldn't have your few and leave it at that, you were somehow weak. You lacked willpower. I didn't get the impression that my dad was indifferent to alcohol: he clearly loved it and the effect it had on him, but he just had the strength of character and resolve to put it down when he needed to. I took this willpower idea to heart, so, in later life, when I found myself waking up in the morning after the night before with a thirst on me and an irresistable compulsion to quench it, I believed that I was simply lacking something. If I gave into temptation, I was very clearly less of a man then my father was. I was morally questionable in some way, bad. I became ashamed of myself and shame is a dangerous game for an addict to play.

But in so many ways, I was lucky to have spent as much time with Pops as I did. I know it's a cliché, but Italia 90 is one of my best sources of childhood memories and a handy little lesson-learner about life. I remember being in town with him in the build-up to the first match and seeing tricolours and green bunting all over Patrick Street, as if we were gearing up for the most extravagant St Patrick's Day bonanza in history. I asked him what was going on and he told me Ireland had qualified for a World Cup for the first time ever. I could see in his face that this was big.

When Lineker fell over himself and into the net to score that terrible opening goal against us in game one my little heart began to break, but in the second half Sheedy brought Cork to a standstill with the equaliser and brought my tough old man to happy sobbing. A 1–1 draw against England: good solid start. In the second game against Egypt, I shared Eamon Dunphy's frustration with our lacklustre performance and actually wandered out onto the street to bang my ball off the wall rather than endure the full second half. Nil-all. I remember thinking that the third game just looked like a bit of craic. I have a memory of the Irish and Dutch players chatting and joking, passing the ball to each other, playing out another draw for a laugh. That was the way it seemed to me, anyway.

And so, to Romania, le crunch. If we got through this, we were into the quarter-finals of the World Cup, which everyone was telling me was absolutely massive and would be Ireland's greatest sporting achievement ever. I didn't know what they were on about because I had just learned 'Jackie's Army', a song which promised we were 'gonna really shake them up when we win the World Cup', so what the big deal was with getting into the quarter-finals I couldn't tell you.

Me and the old man were in Ellis's again. The pub was absolutely jammers but when it got to the penalty shoot-out Dad had me up on his shoulders so I could see, which must've been a source of bitter frustration for the people behind us. As I said, he wasn't really the kind of guy you'd challenge, so we got away with it. When Bonner saved and O'Leary tucked away the winner, the pub became like a WWF (now called WWE) wrestling ring during Royal Rumble. Pints, bottles of Coke, crisps and human bodies were flying everywhere. I went running up and down Gillabbey Street waving a tricolour in my hand, insane with World Cup fever. Grown men and women joined me on the streets. I was the Pied Piper.

For the Italy game, I was up the road in The Rock bar. A seven-year-old on a pub crawl for the boys in green! This experience was more confusing to me than anything else because even though we went 1-0 down, right up until the final minute I had absolute belief that we were going to equalise and then presumably win again on penalties. I had my good runners on and everything and tricolour in hand ready to kick off the street celebrations once more. But the referee blew the final whistle, Italy had beaten Ireland and we were out of the World Cup. Even Jackie Charlton himself, the Jackie of Jackie's Army, was on the pitch waving to the fans, accepting defeat.

I was outraged. I cornered old men in the pub, like my buddy, Wally O'Neill: 'We were supposed to win the thing, Wally, what happened?'

'Ah, that's only a song, little Tadhger,' he laughed.

So, it had all been a ruse. The writers of the song had lied. My anger turned to tears and I cried myself to sleep that night. Italia 90 taught me a number of things: adults lie, particularly in catchy World Cup anthems; the best way to mark achievements or special occasions is to get drunk for weeks on end and, finally, I absolutely loved Ireland.

Chapter Two

My Mother's Keeper

I suppose one day in particular kind of sums the woman up for me. It was the occasion of my first Holy Communion, a bit of a big deal in late-1980s Catholic Ireland. I was seven and dressed in a small man's suit from St Vincent de Paul. I remember feeling pretty cocksure in it to be honest and was really looking forward to showing off to my mam. I strutted down the back garden to her, proud as a peacock. Of course, she was lying down on the grass, locked out of her mind, head buried in a load of piss-in-the-beds. Party on! What a character. I said, 'I made the ol' Communion there today, Mam. Are you proud of me? Do I look nice? Am I your special little soldier?'

And I'll never forget what she said, you know? It was actually just one of those golden, golden moments. She just cocked one eye open and glanced up at me, tear in the eye, grass all over her face, and goes: 'Who are you? Who are you, like? D'ya know? What a messer.' She knew well who I was!

From *In One Eye, Out the Other*

I somehow knew I'd end up writing about my mother one day. Not because I believed I was a brilliant writer and the world simply needed to bear witness to my origin story; it was more that my mother always seemed to me like a character in a book. A complex character, one who you never really knew right up until the end if she was a goody or a baddy. She'd play the innocent but was as cute as a fox. Even as I write these words I can hear her in my head now, 'Don't disgrace me, do you hear me?' She was very committed to keeping the dysfunction within the house private. The house was a zoo, she was the zookeeper, but there were strictly no visitors. I think about her a lot. I still dream about her regularly. I love her, I resent her – or, at least, I used to, bitterly. I felt like she was wilfully driving me insane and yet she was probably the only person in the world I could rely on for practical comfort and security, a bed for the night and a roof over my head when I'd burned all the bridges during my own battles with addiction. I will not do her justice but let me tell you about my mother.

Even a foolish fool as foolhardy as yours fooly knew that I was clearly another one of Ireland's great 'mistakes'. My sister vaguely recalls that when my mother was expecting me, she spent most of the time in an acute state of anxiety. She was forty, a gossip-worthy ripe old age to be popping out another sprog in 1980s Ireland. She worried constantly that there would be complications with the pregnancy and the birth, and, though she had a generally cataclysmic outlook, in this instance her fears were reasonable. Giving birth to her last boy, my brother Con, and the aftermath of that probably changed her forever. So, like the political philosopher Thomas Hobbes, whose frightened mother delivered him into the world with the Anglo-Spanish War starting up outside the window, I, too, was born in fear. If you think that's a pretentious and random comparison, I'm only warming up.

I did get the tail end of the charismatic, roguish, sociable person she apparently once was. She was a striking-looking woman with high cheekbones. As a kid, I remember her coming into the kitchen with the shopping and her long, fawn Macintosh coat whooshing after her and the accompanying feeling of contentment – 'Ah, nice one, my mam's home.' I wonder what treats she's after getting me, I'd think.

There were varying accounts of the story but my mam always said when my dad first met her on her street (his buddy was going out with her older sister) he was smitten, but she was going out with someone else who was equally lovestruck. My father's persistence paid off because Mam cruelly stood the other lad up one night and the wheels were set in motion for Cork to have its spiritual leader, a boy child named Tadhg (same number of letters as 'Jesus'. Weird, isn't it?) born in Erinville Hospital one glorious summer's afternoon in July in 1982. Mam's account of their early courtship was that Dad was lucky to bag this absolute stunner and boy did he know it; Dad's assessment was that 'you wouldn't get her [Mam] in a lucky bag'. But he was merely being playful. He certainly loved her and she him; before she got lost in herself, there was a lot to love.

I was sure that she loved me, that was never in doubt. I think the problem with Mam was that she loved wrong. She thought 'love' meant protecting me from the world, or maybe protecting me while I protected her. My sister recalls me being strapped into some class of a high chair at three or four years of age for hours on end. She, in all seriousness, suggested fitting me with a permanent indoor helmet until my father stepped in. My mother's obsession with keeping me out of harm's way, however oppressive or bizarre the methods, went unchallenged. My older brothers used to take the piss out of her and me for the Oedipus-in-chains routine.

I was the favourite and, looking back on it, that was the worst place to be. All her anxieties, fears and foibles, barely under wraps for the first forty years of her life, seemed to burst out of the traps after I came along. And if you indulge me with the greyhound-racing analogy a moment longer, I was the plastic hare. My brother Con, twelve years my senior, had, to quote my mother, 'been born perfect', without any medical anomalies but he had some minor health issues and while in hospital contracted meningitis. The result was my mam sitting alone in a cold room in the hospital listening to the equally cold words of the specialist: 'You do realise you are rearing a vegetable?'

Whether my brother was born with intellectual and physical challenges or meningitis caused them is hard to say for sure. I know that sounds fucking awful and I feel queasy writing it, but the fact of the matter is Mam was a bit of a *seanachaí*. Not an adorable, brilliant, bearded one, more like one who invents versions of stories to elicit sympathy or, better still, spark a bit of drama and get her family warring with each other. She'd commit to her stories so completely I'd imagine truth and fiction must have become blurred to her, as they did for her kids. She'd regularly tell me that my sister had been complaining about me when she wouldn't have said a thing, and in later years, when my brothers came to visit, she'd hit them with a list of things me and my sister had supposedly said they should be doing for Mam but weren't. The result was that we kids sometimes treated each other with unfounded suspicion and resentment. Classic divide and conquer. Often she'd just lie out of boredom or because the truth didn't quite suit her. She was very proud of me for getting into University College Cork – even putting my exam results in the parish news-letter – but my chosen degree of English Literature and Philosophy sounded a bit wishy-washy to her ears. The nail in the coffin was when her sister, whom she wanted to impress more than anyone else on earth, skeptically asked her, 'Would you ever tell me, what's philosophy?' Fast-forward a couple of years and I'm visiting cousins in England I hadn't met since I was a kid. One of them asks me one evening, 'How are you finding your law degree, very demanding course I'm told?' Oh very demanding, especially when you're at Existentialism lectures or in the college bar all day. Mumsie thought 'Law' sounded a bit better so decided to tweak my story without telling me. That was a theme.

Irrespective of precisely when and how Con's difficulties began, the thought of her in that room on her own hearing the news delivered that way by some dickhead specialist makes my heart break. The result was Con spent his life confined to a chair and, especially early on, was prone to the most horrific epileptic seizures you can imagine. I can only speculate but I'd imagine this pushed her over the edge from eccentric and nervy to agoraphobic, obsessive-compulsive and chronically anxious.

Rather understandably for somebody with a latent and then overt panic disorder, Mam believed that I was about to follow Con's path at any moment. I was regularly taken out of primary school at yard time, which was a source of much frustration to me seeing as I was a tasty little soccer player. Little did I know things were to get much worse. By fourth class, she'd started to randomly keep me off school for periods of time, sometimes weeks. She'd tell me I was sick. I'd sometimes have a mild cold but as time went on, I didn't have to have any symptoms at all. I'd spend the day with her watching *Neighbours* and *Going for Gold*. Flip side, my knowledge of European capital cities was sensational for a ten-year-old and I've Henry Kelly to thank for that.

When I dig deep and really go down memory lane it's genuinely shocking for me to recall that my father had to have known some if not all of what was going on. I have a clear memory of sitting down watching an episode of *Cheers* one night having been out of school for several days, if not weeks. My viewing pleasure was interrupted by my dad frustratedly writing out a series of sums that I was supposed to do to keep up with my schoolwork while I was on this hiatus. If I knew I wasn't sick, he must have too. He didn't seem best pleased but as far as I can remember he didn't challenge her. It was bizarre because he had an incredibly strong work ethic and I'd have thought a guy lounging around in his pyjamas watching TV when he should be at school would have been anathema to him. She was his blind spot, I guess. I actually started to wonder if maybe I was sick and I just didn't realise it. She'd also encourage me to tell her stories, often made-up ones from school involving the other kids in my class and teachers. I have memories of being in her bed telling her stories, making her laugh, soothing her before sleep. I became a talking security blanket.

At the end of fourth class, my teacher handed out prizes for the best boys in the class. I think I came second and bagged myself a nifty paint set. I was delighted with myself until Mr Lynch made a speech about me. 'Tadhg Hickey's award is a special one. It is an extraordinary achievement for him to have done so well in his exams especially as he missed so much time this year due to illness. I want everyone to give him a clap.' My joy seemed to ebb away and give way to a not-so-new feeling: shame. I hadn't been sick; I didn't deserve this pity. This wasn't right but what was I going to do? Tell

Lynchy that I wasn't sick, I was actually just at home helping my mam feel OK?

As my mother withdrew further and further, the house became untidy and so did I. My sister, only a few years older than me, increasingly became my mother, washing my manky hair and whatnot, making me food; although, to be fair, my dad did a lot of that too. Before my mother's agoraphobia overwhelmed her, she would still go shopping and then to the pub with my dad afterwards. On these occasions, my sister, just a child herself, would mind me. I'm great craic as you know, but that must have been such a drag for a kid.

Although I didn't make the connection at the time, on reflection now and with the help of a crack team of therapists, I have begun to connect my own anxiety to my mother's. I remember one time as a kid playing soccer just down the road from my house with a load of other lads. It was a summer's day and my mam came out to the front gate and called me in. I assumed she was just reminding me to drink some water as the other parents did but she was actually calling me in for the day. She wanted me to stop playing football. I said that it was early and that everyone else was out, what was the problem? She said, 'But your father is out fishing and I'm here on my own. I've no one to talk to.'

I intuitively knew there was something wrong about our relationship but I didn't get angry, not yet. I felt so sorry for her – here she was on a beautiful summer's day trapped in her own house, clearly fearful, with no one by her side. I felt that my dad was trying his best to ignore the worst of her behaviour and that I should somehow try to fix or certainly mollify her. I began to take on the fear that consumed her, like it was a contagion. I seemed to now feel her sadness, feel her worry. I'd no business playing football: there was a situation here and I was needed. I would choose neither fight nor flight. (I actually didn't realise there were other options until Bubbsie, my therapist, pointed it out to me recently.) Instead, I fawned. I thought it was my job to make my mam's worries go away. If I came up with one of my crazy stories about building a spaceship out of Cornflakes boxes and empty toilet rolls and getting ill-advised space launches going in the garden, she would start to feel better and then, hopefully, I would too.

On reflection, Mam probably had a plethora of undiagnosed mental health issues. There was certainly depression and anxiety, agoraphobia, as I say, which grew worse and worse throughout my formative years, and the most obvious of all: OCD. Every night she'd tap the knobs on the cooker, flick the power switch on and off, and tap the handles on the locked doors a specific number of times in sequence before she went to bed. It used to drive my father crazy but I'm not sure if any of us took it seriously enough. We could have done a lot more to help her rather than just enable her, but the big problem was I don't remember her recognising that there was a problem to solve. In her mind, the world was an endlessly dangerous place, threats were everywhere and your best bet was to stay inside with your mam, locking doors, tapping cooker knobs and telling her stories.

She accepted help with the particularly jagged edges of her anxiety. For this she used Valium, with mixed results, but around the time I began secondary school, she found a new infinitely more effective solution to her disease: booze, glorious booze. And then, all hell broke loose.

She had drunk for years, largely sociably, always at weekends and never would have seen herself as having a problem. Her self-imposed lockdown had separated her from social drinking for a number of years by now and then one night my dad brought her home a few cans after work and she drank them. The experiment went so well, it started to become a regular thing every weekend and, in no time at all, the cans started appearing on week-days too. Inside a year or so, bottles of whiskey entered the fray. In hindsight, her accelerated descent into alcoholic drinking makes so much sense to me. A chronically anxious person with a perpetual racing brain discovers heavy drinking and suddenly feels like the world can go and worry about itself. Of course you're going to get addicted to that. And naturally, it was a hard sell for the family to say, we'd like you to stop. What was she going back to? Sitting on the chair in a world of her own making in great psychological distress, now with no effective anaesthetic?

Obviously, this is all in hindsight. At the time I just didn't understand why my mother seemed to be hellbent on breaking my spirit. Her drunkenness made me feel that pesky shame again: I was never able to have friends over and was constantly careful what I told people about my mam. One time I accidentally said too much to a friend's mother who read between the lines and got some sense of what was going on at home, but as soon as she started talking about intervening or trying to help me in some way, I backtracked, became cold and never allowed the topic of my mother to come up again. Who was this hoity-toity middle-class mum to judge my mother? Alright, Mam was an absolute basket case driving me to within an inch of my sanity but she was *my* basket case and we keep our problems to ourselves, thank you very much. I'll say the most heinous things I want about my family to my family, but God help you if you criticise them.

Watching her drunk and listening to her incoherent *ráiméising* was not the worst of it. You could always slam the door on her, run upstairs, put on your Doors albums and forget your troubles. But when the falling started, we descended to a new Dantean circle. At this point (I was fifteen), it was just myself and my sister at home and, as I say, my dad had a bit of a hear-no-evil thing going on with Mam. He worked and if he wasn't, he'd be gardening, fishing, occasionally drinking – anything to get a breather from her, I'd imagine. I was longing for breathers myself. It was extremely difficult to have anything approaching a reasonable conversation with her by this point. If she was sober, she'd be so anxious and on edge that she'd mostly just be interrogating you to see if you'd pulled out plugs, locked windows, etc. If you were going anywhere, she'd warn of the risks she'd heard about on the radio; threats were everywhere and imminent.

My mother was overweight and riddled with arthritis. She hadn't done any of the exercises necessary to stave off the worst of the inflammation and hadn't taken a lot of the medications either, for fear of them interacting badly with the booze. So instead, she would just get tanked up and semi-regularly fall over. In the kitchen, bathroom, in the front garden a couple of times. The night before my Junior Cert English exam, I sat by her side in the kitchen because she'd fallen with her head lodged up against the back door. I couldn't lift her on my own, my sister was out, I can't remember where my dad was, so I just sat there listening to her babbling, cursing her I suppose, feeling really sorry for myself. And if I'm to really dig deep – I kind of liked it as well.

The next day, all the family would be sure to gather and the talk would be that it was awful that I was left on my own with her, what she was doing to the family, particularly to me, was unacceptable. Fair play to me for doing my exams, etc. I'd enjoy the attention. In my head, I was quietly becoming a bit of a martyr and I was unconsciously storing up these traumatic events – I didn't know why I was pocketing them but later on they were wonderful excuses when I went missing for days and started treating people like shit myself. Or maybe it was more of the dissociation that had served me so well as a little kid. I'm not here, my mother isn't face down with her head almost lodged between the cupboard and the cooker, this is not my life.

Trauma is a bitch, though, it's like running up a tab. If you've got an obliging barman, you can do it problem-free for a long time but you know the day is coming when you're going to run out of wriggle room and the bill will have to be paid. I remember specifically one time watching her lying in the muck and flowers and grass in the front garden, feeling that the image itself was damaging me as I stood there looking at it, twisting my mind or something. I can't remember how we got her in the house that day, almost certainly my sister was involved, but I do remember running upstairs and jotting some notes in my diary. I wrote that I didn't think I'd be able to manage too many more days like that one. I was OK with sadness but I was terrified of losing my mind. And I suppose I was also simply scared of losing my mother.

And yet these big traumatic events were a kind of a release in a strange way. You knew when a fall or some other calamitous event was coming and you almost welcomed it because in the short term it would lead to a reduction or elimination of alcohol (due to the fear of falling again) and also the wider family would be more likely to step in and share the burden. Plus, I'd get lots of, 'Sure, God love poor Tadhg.'

It seemed as if me, my sister and Mam were trapped in this weird and wearying *Glass Menagerie* reboot – a frightened and embittered matriarch trying desperately to cling onto and control her youngest children by entombing them in her own neuroses. If we got job opportunities, she would congratulate us out of one side of her mouth and then caution us that we were probably about to be made fools of from the other side. She urged me not to leave Cork (to be fair, it's hard to argue with her on this point) – she was preoccupied with the idea that if I went somewhere else, say for instance Dublin, I was sure to be stabbed, beaten up or sexually assaulted. Her already anxious and cynical worldview was reinforced by her daytime television intake of *Jerry Springer*, *Judge Judy* and RTÉ news. If I was out in college or at work, she would ring me, sometimes several times a day, mostly just to confirm that I was still alive.

The mixture of the constant surveillance, the infectious anxiety, the dreary world view and then the active alcoholism as the cherry on top created in me a sense of desperation to break out, to finally free myself from the high chair and to encounter for the first time real freedom. But a major barrier was that I loved my sister and she loved me and we had an unspoken pact. We were comrades in a long drawn-out war to defend our marbles. I couldn't go on without her.

I also wouldn't have had a clue what to do or where to go. I was scared to leave the family home and Cork, truth be told. I don't think I'm being too harsh on myself when I say I was a pretty useless young fella. At this stage, I was eighteen going on thirteen; I'd no interest in learning any life skills, really. I relied on the benevolence of friends to help apply for part-time work: to this day, I have an irrational beef with forms. I never showed any interest in learning to drive or cook or do anything that amounted to looking after oneself. I had quintessential arrested development. And certainly after I started drinking, a big part of me stopped growing. At eighteen, I knew how to pass exams, deal with a bananas mother (or so I thought) and get wrecked. That was enough to be getting on with.

Chapter Three

The Boy with the Exploding Head

From a young age I realised that my brain was kind of 'weird'. But it didn't really bother me much. From as early as I can remember, I had the perception that there were board meetings going on in my head before and after I made decisions. To me, it was because they were vital decisions with potentially global significance but looking back on it they were probably about what type of wrestling figure I'd try to petition my dad to buy me on Saturday afternoon. I remember telling my sister about the board meeting thing. I could see in her face a mash-up of mild admiration and concern. Which again was fine by me because at the same time as being anxious, I was a fairly happy-go-lucky kid. As a smallie, doing a lot of my growing up in pubs with my mam and dad, I'd often be found playing darts or pool with ol' lads, grabbing the mic and singing rebel songs at weddings and funerals, playing football on the street with my buddies, obsessing about the Irish soccer team's treacherous qualification journey to USA '94 with tricky away ties in Albania, Lithuania and Latvia. I didn't spend much time in dark rooms staring into space in the throes of existential crises. The mental-health thing is so nuanced.

Sometimes I wasn't in good form, though. The concept of moods fascinated me then as it does now. I was playing soccer in the garden once, I must have been about six or seven, and just sensing this wave of glumness wash over me. I felt a nervousness in my legs and I immediately stopped playing. I looked around me and to the sky. Had something changed? Were other people experiencing this unpleasant shift? I'm just trying to finish a game of World Cup here, this is lousy. The best way I can describe it is that there were times or periods when it felt like I felt too much. Everything was dialled up just that little bit too far. This feeling of not quite being able to take the intensity of what I was experiencing in my life created, or perhaps itself became, a symptom of severe anxiety. Of course, I wouldn't have named it that at the time. I remember as a little kid going to the toilet alone, feeling distressed, and thinking, *my head might be about to burst.* It felt hot, like a pressure cooker of boiling potatoes and somebody needed to take the screw off, let a bit of whistling steam out. As terrified as I was, I was a rational little weirdo in my own way and I thought to myself, *I can't let my head explode all over the toilet without letting anyone know. I better inform my mam and hopefully we'll take steps together to manage the imminent explosion as best we can.*

I walked out into the living room and momentarily doubted myself. I was afraid of being shunned or maybe even locked away if I explained it in the terms that seemed most apt to me. I decided to present it in a manner in which I felt my mother would accept it. 'Mam, my head feels hot and I feel too sad to do my maths homework.'

I remember her laughing, actually guffawing, saying something like, 'Go way now, boy, I'm not bad enough without listening to that!' She might have taken it as some sort of strange joke, which, to be fair, I was prone to. But I decided there and then: when it comes to the really wacky, troubling stuff going on inside the noggin, the really deep-seated, crazy-town stuff – keep that to yourself, Tadhger.

I wouldn't have realised it at the time but beneath all the weird thoughts and unpleasant sensations, the thing that underpinned and indeed created all of them, was good old-fashioned fear. I've yet to meet a person struggling with addiction or another mental illness who doesn't experience extraordinary, seemingly inexplicable fear, from the time they enter the world. In my case, I experienced fear as an alien force, this external thing that for some reason invaded my spirit at inopportune moments, like when trying to finish a game of World Cup in the garden. I wasn't a disturbed young fella running around pulling holy pictures off the wall. The fear came and went but I was baffled by it and ashamed of it. One time I was watching Italian soccer with my dad upstairs and he went to get something out of the shed. I remember listening carefully and the time going by so slowly.

What could be keeping him? He should be back by now, I thought. I wasn't three or four when this happened, more like nine or ten. A cascade of anxious thoughts pummelled me. *What if he's been abducted? What if he's dead? What'll I do? What if I die with the fright? What if I live but my life falls apart without my dad?* Next thing, I can't breathe. I'm in full-on panic mode, flying down the stairs and running into the kitchen, to see my dad re-emerge from the shed looking at me oddly, going, 'What's wrong?'

Don't tell them about the weird stuff. 'Nothing – just wanted to tell you Inter Milan are on.'

And the fear was so visceral. I couldn't ignore it. It was a feeling of impending catastrophe, misplaced excitement in the depths of my stomach and a headache from the overthinking. Then it would pass. I'd be like, 'What the fuck was that?' to myself. I'd go play some football or listen to my sister's record collection or eat a packet of custard creams – because it's worth noting that, towards the end of primary school, I was (unknowingly) comfort eating the shit out of it.

Usually the fear was precipitated by this profound, hard-to-remove feeling in the pit of my stomach or soul. One of my childhood heroes, Jim Morrison of The Doors, described it better than most: 'Something wrong, something not quite right.' I mean, how would you even articulate that to someone if you wanted to? It was early-to-mid-nineties Ireland. There were no Blindboys or Russell Brands. The only time you'd hear about mental health was when newscasters would throw it in at the end of a description of a frenzied murder or something. I thought it best to live with the sporadic discomfort in my head and hope that it just went away by itself: psychotherapy and spiritual healing, Irish style.

I became fat. Is it OK to say that about yourself? When I was in primary school, I was a huge little guy. Lunch every day: three egg-and-cheese sandwiches. When I'd get home from school – and I'm not joking you here – before dinner, I'd have a big bowl of Frosties . . . with sugar. The Frostie, as you might know, is weighed down with sugar. Not enough for me. And when I say big bowl, I'd like you to picture one of those fruit bowls you'd see in the lobby of an old-fashioned hotel, well capable of housing a melon and an assortment of large oranges. Yes, that's the lad. That's what I thought was normal. How do you know what's normal or not till people tell ya?

I was so rotund I had to get my pants specially made for me. The next-door neighbour was a tailor, which was pretty handy when you were a seam-buster, like myself. 'Do you know where your pants come from?' my sister cautiously asked me one time.

'Ya, Mr O'Connor makes 'em,' I replied. 'Who cares?'

I knew I was a big lad and that I was eating a lot but I wasn't too bothered. Those egg-and-cheese sambos and buckets of Frosties were damn tasty, and being a bit out of breath playing soccer and having a set of what I think they call moobs these days seemed a small price to pay to keep them in my life. I do remember feeling embarrassed one time in school when I walked into the toilet and a couple of bigger lads were in there. I'd a Batman T-shirt underneath my school shirt and one of the lads shouted, 'Batman, haha! More like Fatman.' Not a bad gag in hindsight but at the time, that shit hurts. I came back from the toilet, sat down at my desk, put my sloppy, chubby hand under my chins and looked out the window forlornly. The Charlie Brown routine caught teacher's eye.

You know when you're young and there's this one teacher? Mrs C had blonde, TV-commercial hair and looked a bit like Princess Diana, I thought. And her perfume, oh my God. You know that perfect age when sex hasn't even occurred to you yet, it's just love. You're just plain in love with your teacher. Me and Mrs C 'always and 4eva'. I'm a grossly overweight, very confused eight-year-old and she's a married school teacher in her early forties but as far as I'm concerned, we're gonna make it! All I want to do is just go for walks with her, smell her perfume as she leans over me to correct my homework and buy her a few buns at the cake sale.

So, she was standing there and she asked me, 'Are you OK, Tadhg?'

I was thinking of something to say without admitting 'not really, I've just found out I'm a beast'. So I said, 'Eh, ya, just some guys in sixth class mocked my Batman T-shirt.'

'They're just jealous,' she said. Now, the t-shirt was readily available to all and sundry retailing at a competitive £6.99 in Dunnes Stores, but I could see what Mrs C was trying to do here and it was kinda working: 'They just want to be a superhero like you.' Maybe, Mrs C, maybe.

I make light of the overeating but I suppose if I really drill into it, I was surely stuffing my gob to swallow my feelings. Mam rarely left the house and every moment I spent there was usually with her. But even though I often felt anxious with and for her, there was an attractive lawlessness, which she presided over: as long as I was spending time with her, I could do what I wanted. I could eat the whole packet of custard creams for dinner, I could stay home from school – why not? There were no rules, except one: look after your mam. Pops didn't rock the boat, so the biscuits kept coming.

By the age of twelve I was distracting myself not just with custard creams but with books. I loved poetry and plays. You could get lost in those bad boys. They made me feel alive and connected. I loved Shakespeare, or Willy Shakes as my buddy E in school used to call him. E stood up one day in the middle of English class in a bid to run down the clock and declared, 'Ah, sir, Shakespeare. He's one of the greats, really, isn't he?'

My exasperated teacher said, 'E, I know what you're trying to do, sit down and get on with it.'

E doubled down: 'Ah, sir, let's call a spade a spade. Has to be one of the greats if not *THE* great!'

'Get out!' That teacher, Mr O'K, kickstarted my life-long love of literature, actually. And he'd also offer me unexpected, extraordinary solidarity in my hour of need.

Ironically, in spite of not attending very often, I liked school a lot. Very early on I comprehended that second-ary school in particular was a game of survival and it was imperative to learn the rules and perfect techniques to ensure you made it through. I liked that. I liked the challenge of it. And challenges were everywhere.

I left primary school as one of the top kids in the class. Because of my weird board-meeting mind and other flights of fancy bouncing around my head, I was under the impression that I must be a brilliant child. There was a child prodigy doing the rounds on the telly at the time. He had a posh English accent, dressed in tweed, wore a monocle and was an expert on antiques and ancient Greek and Roman literature. He was my boy. I'd prob-ably be shunned by the other kids but lauded by the teachers when I arrived at the gates of Spioraid Naoimh to start my secondary school education. It was really quite mortifying to learn that in actual fact, I was bang average. Certainly well behind in Irish, with no discern-ible flair for mathematics, only capable of mixing it with the big boys in English and history. Same with sports. I left Glasheen as easily the best soccer player in the class, chubby as I was. I had a wicked way with an orange cup champions ball on a wet or sleety yard. I was touted as being the next Liam 'Chippy' Brady with my cultured left foot and a lazy, mercurial style (I may have driven or even created this touting). Again, first kickabout in secondary school I fell on my arse after attempting to do a trick I taught myself from a Pelé video. From what I can remember, the video was produced after Pelé threw his lot in with Pfizer in putting Viagra on the map. So I'd say his head was elsewhere. RIP.

OK, I'm not the smartest anymore, not the best soccer player, what can I excel at to make me bullyproof and ensure these six years are pain free, I wondered. The ideal scenario, as far as I could see, was to be loved by all. And so began a lifelong commitment to people-pleasing.

I would sit eating my egg sandwiches in the lunchroom telling wacky stories and doing weird voices for a couple of equally confused-as-to-what-they-were-supposed-to-be kids. In time, the stories grew and so did the audience. I recall one lunch where maybe a dozen kids had gathered around waiting for me to say or do something humorous. Evidence was mounting that the one thing that seemed to unite kids of all gangs and persuasions was having a laugh. The joker was the safest card in the pack.

I'd no idea that I wanted to be a comedian when I was a nipper. But jokes, characters, weird voices, phrases and language were part of the fabric of my life. Comedy came naturally but I wouldn't have called it that. From early on, me and my sister used jokes to deal with the fact that our mother was neglectful and mentally unstable. Jet-black humour, Irish style. But I didn't need Bill Hicks or Lenny Bruce for my early laughs. My taste was broad and unpredictable. My sister recalls being upstairs in the house and hearing me downstairs in the living room reeling in laughter, doubled over, punching the ground in a life-threatening fit of giggles. Opening the living-room door, she was surprised to see me incapacitated by none other than Benny Hill. Hill's hilarious high jinks – which I assume involved him running away from some awkward situation or other, pursued by an assortment of scantily-clad women – had almost been the death of me. In my defence, I was six or seven years old.

My first joke was characteristically political but, on reflection, lacked even the most basic tenets of a well-constructed gag. It went as follows:

'Knock knock.'
'Who's there?'
'Maggie.'
'Maggie who?'
'Maggie Thatcher.'

At the time, I thought the serviceable 'knock knock' joke needed only to conceal the second part (or indeed, in this case, name) until the punchline. You can understand my confusion: every time I cracked this joke adults would laugh and even clap yet nobody pointed out the basic flaw. If only we'd had Twitter in the late 1980s.

Benny Hill notwithstanding, as a kid my comedy heroes were not so much nuanced, cerebral stand-ups like

Stewart Lee; I was more attracted to comedic madmen who seemed to be risking life and limb to make me laugh. Rik Mayall, John Cleese, Chevy Chase – madness and comedy intertwined, egging each other on, that was my poison. And for as long as I can remember, jokes were just roaming round my head all day long. Regardless of what situation I'm in, I'm always thinking, 'Why is this funny?' Because it usually is, because everything is funny. It's not that I'm trying to generate material for a sketch or stand-up routine; I'm thinking like this because I have to, I've no choice – they're automatic thoughts. I'm not saying I'm a brilliant comedian or even a good one – all I'm saying is that I am one. I've a joker's soul. I can't help it.

Perhaps it's important to say it in a comedian's memoir about alcoholism and mental illness: having a laugh was there long before alcohol and, thankfully, it's been there long afterwards. I've heard Damien Dempsey and many others talk about music's ability to soothe the troubled kid. Well, comedy did that for me: watching one of my faves or, better still, retiring to the front room with an old-school ghetto blaster and a blank tape to record comedy talk shows, playing all the characters. I couldn't give a damn what was going on around me when I was in joke world and, as my friends and family can attest, that is still the case today.

The joking around seemed to ease my inadequacies both at school and in the family. My older brothers, Declan and Alan, were taller, more muscular than me, handy with their fists, old-school working men. I, on the other hand (pun intended) had the hands of a ballerina, the rough and readiness of Marie Antoinette, and the fighting skills of a duck. If they were up trees cutting branches to beat the head off each other with, I was under that tree, reading Keats. This was the perennial dichotomy of my life and identity. My family partly saw me as a pseudo-bourgeois little upstart, yet later in university and particularly the theatre circles I mixed in, I saw myself as a much maligned working-class hero. A 'Marx on the Lee', rallying the proletariat, agitating for change, usually demented on a cocktail of drink, drugs and Wikipedia.

I loved Keats from a young age and didn't give a shit about that being uncool. I loved the way poetry could just make you feel all that love and sadness and beauty that the poet had burned onto the page. I particularly liked the sadness. I was greatly look-ing forward to getting dumped by my first love so I could lock myself away with some country music and the complete works of Keats. First, I had to find my first love. Little did I know that she only lived out the Lough, a hop, skip and a swan ride from my house in McCurtain Villas.

I first met Grace at an ice-cream shop, where I would assume most great romantic adventures begin. We were both about ten or eleven years old. I was buying an ice cream; she was buying a Mr Freeze. The conversation went something like this:

G: I think I know your mam

T: Ya, I think my mam knows your mam.

G: Anyway, do you live up there?

T: Ya. Do you live down through there?

G: Ya. K, see ya.

T: Bye.

Perfunctory, introductory, but laced with amorous tension. To my young heart, I was Joyce, she was Nora Barnacle and we had exchanged the most vital, potent, earth-shattering expressions of love known to McCurtain Villas, Greenmount, Bandon Road and the Lough combined. She had big brown eyes and sallow skin and looked the bop off the nerdy Winnie from *The Wonder Years*.

I walked back home in stunned silence, the 99 destroying my fat little hand (again) and causing a sticky mess inside my fingers. Was she my girlfriend now? Would we have to leave our foolish, childish ways behind us and start a life elsewhere? (I still had Winnie in my head and assumed that Grace was the studious type.) We'd retire to a cabin in the forest where she would read the classics for the day while I would chop firewood and hunt bears, and in the evenings we'd sit by the sea (in my head there was a sea in the middle of the forest), watch the sun go down, eating our Mr Freezes and 99s. In this fantasy sequence, I didn't spill a drop (like my dad) and my hands weren't small and fat with cocktail sausages for fingers. They were massive and brutish like Fionn mac Cumhaill's. Was

I running away with myself? Were things moving too fast or maybe not fast enough? Did I risk losing her if I didn't take action right away?

In the weeks that followed, I engineered a lot of the soccer matches and shenanigans with my buddies to be nearer and nearer Grace's house, and, hey presto, in no time at all, Grace and her two friends were regularly hanging out with me and my buddies, A and L. Once I got past the initial terror, I became the star performer for my team. Quick with the gags, breaking the tension. During one-to-one time with Grace, I'd crack out a bit of a sonnet or a spot of Keats, about which she was might-ily impressed. Not living up to her Winnie comparison, Grace had actually lost her English textbook and had brazenly neglected to replace it. A James Dean type, love it. That's my girl.

The other lads started asking me for advice on how to talk to the ladies. 'Just relax, lads, just be yourself, yeah? If I know women like I think I know them, they don't want a desperate man. Play it cool.'

It was all building towards a magic night in August when, as the whispers and rumours had it, we were going to go around the back of the church with each other. It was kind of assumed that I'd be going with Grace as I clearly had the pick of them and Grace was my long-standing fave and soon-to-be forest-cabin wifey and soulmate. I'd been listening to Mike + the Mechanics and the Bangles all summer and it all seemed to be writ-ten in the stars. L, perhaps the second most appealing in the group after me, not looking too dissimilar from Grace actually, with his own set of brown eyes and sallow skin, was sure to head off with Grace's bestie, Lara. And A and Michelle would complete the series.

As we walked up through the grounds of the Lough church, I felt nervous but focused. I'd never kissed anyone before but, really, what was there to be so scared about? Me and my Grace clearly loved and cherished each other deeply and now was simply the time to seal the deal with a kiss. When we arrived at the scene the girls seemed a bit coy. The ease and playfulness of the summer had evaporated and now a weird, tense *Judgement-Day* energy prevailed. To cut the tension, L said, 'I'll just go up and ask Grace for you, will I?' *Nice one, L*, I thought. *Start with the obvious and work your way down.* One quick last sniff of each armpit, a couple of chewing-gum golf balls lobbed in the gob and here we go. Showtime.

L approached Grace awkwardly. 'Will you meet Tadhg?' he mumbled. There was a beat. It was long. *Oh shit, it's too long*, I thought. Finally, Grace said: 'Tadhg? Nooo!' laughing loudly. She even looked at me as she was laughing, as if it was a completely ridiculous, practically unworkable notion.

Never show what's going on. I laughed back, 'Hahahaha.' What a big laugh! As if me and Grace were going to score with each other, like. Sure, we're just great friends. We'd have no business starting a family in a forest. L came back to me with a pain on his face that seemed to be easing, watching me laugh. 'Would it be OK if I scored with her, so? She just asked me there.'

Of course. Go round the back of the church there and take a machete to my heart, hopes and dreams.

Chapter Four

Gatman Begins

Wet brain, like. Dunno if you know it? Nasty stuff. You push the drinkin' too far and you could end up back like you're a child again (long, awkward beat). Which would be great for me, 'cause I never actually managed to make the ol' communion! I wouldn't mind another go off it. I was so nervous when the priest was coming along the rail of the Lough Church, that when he goes 'Body of Christ?', I'd my uncle in my head and I goes, 'Nah, boy, eatin's cheatin',' and I downed his goblet of wine. I suppose that was the start of it, as the fella says!

From *In One Eye, Out the Other*

In spite of the fact that I was captivated by pubs and pub culture when I was still only in short pants, taking the leap to drinking myself still felt enormous, almost insurmountable. When the childhood friends got to about fifteen, a few of them started drinking and I was transfixed. It was hard to say no because I had built this persona (based on absolutely nothing) that I was a gag-cracking, tough-talking, ladies-getting Renaissance man. That I would fall at the first major hurdle in our journey into adulthood was incongruous with that image. But I knew, deep down inside, I wasn't ready.

I thought of myself then, and still do today, as an easy-going guy. I'll happily let someone else order for me in a restaurant, as long as they know I hate mushrooms. (I've a serious issue with mushrooms – the way they kind of burst in your mouth is simply hideous. Like little grey animal testicles in a bush-tucker trial. Yock. I don't mind the magic ones though. More on that later.) People can change plans on me, I barely notice. And yet in times of crisis, the unmerciful control freak in me comes out. I wasn't ready for putting on shirts and Brylcreem and Lynx Africa. I wasn't ready for chatting to girls in nightclubs. I wasn't ready for nightclubs. I had become comfortable in my not-yet-drinkin', watching *Match of the Day* on a Saturday night. Playing football till all hours, watching reruns of comedies on RTÉ (it used to be good when I was a kid, believe it or not!) on a Friday night, more football Saturday morning with Casement Celtic, messing in school, filling my friends' heads full of shit with stories about all the crazy debauchery I got up to on the last family holiday – which, needless to say, we never took. That was my world. I understood that world. I was the king of that castle; I was happy to look out from behind the walls but scared to confront the imminent threats on the horizon.

So, I thought, the best thing to do was to split the group in two. The younger teetotallers, led by me, would shun the older drinking boys, like the pioneers of the prohibition movement in the US or the young fanatical

Father Mathew, the Temperance priest who tried to rid Cork of gargle. I attempted to create a subculture of happily sober teenagers around Barrack Street, College Road and Greenmount, all because I was scared I didn't fully understand how to kiss. Or that I would be spurned again, as I had been on the grounds of the Lough church. Or, worse again, that I wouldn't be able to handle drink and go mad or something.

I came from drinkers. I knew that world intimately, long before I drank. Drink was what brought family and the community together. And it was good clean fun a lot of the time, or at least that was the way it seemed to me as a kid in the bar. Sing-songs, Ireland matches and pool tournaments were great craic. But as I grew older, I started to notice the casualties. Vibrant lads who used to lead the merriment in the pub were now losing their jobs, health and families because they couldn't stop drinking. You'd see them on crutches after bad falls or beatings, shuffling into daytime watering holes on Barrack Street, eyes dancing about the place, eager not to be spotted in the liminal space between the fantasy land of the pub and the real world. In time, their eyes stopped dancing as they stopped caring. And at home, of course, it seemed like my mother was losing what was left of her mind because of the stuff. I wanted so badly to drink but I was simultaneously terrified of what exactly would come next. I needed to kick the can down the road for a while.

My plan worked. We distanced ourselves from the drinkers and were never really friends with them again.

In later years, I'd see them out in pubs and clubs and we'd kind of laugh about it, but there was always this weird, unspoken tension. At least, I felt there was. Confronted with the pressure and fear of drinking, I had chosen to shun and hurt people rather than just admit I was scared. I didn't want to be the only one not drinking, so I took hostages and convinced a bunch of kids that they didn't really want to drink either. This type of manipulation technique was learned from the best.

When I was about eleven, me and the folks were gearing up for our first ever holiday outside Ireland. My dad's brother and his family lived in Jersey and my dad had never been to see him before. I could see in him what a big deal this was. My uncle had moved from Mayfield and made a big success of himself in the Channel Islands and my dad was so proud of him. They looked alike and had been inseparable as kids. I was beside myself. I loved planes and airports. I'd been to the airport a handful of times to pick people up but the thought of actually going on a plane myself was keeping me up at night with fever-pitch excitement. A lot of my friends went to Spain every summer and one buddy had even been to the US a couple of times. I was finally about to join the jet-setters. I was going to see what the sun looked like outside Ireland and what the girls looked like too. Our tickets were booked and the July departure date was highlighted, underlined and exclamation-marked on my Credit Union calendar.

My mother let it be known that she was going for us. She had a fear of flying and, by this stage, socialising, and it was very clear to me just how grateful we should be for this act of self-sacrifice on her part. However, in early June, she had a conversation with someone who told her that the plane to and from Jersey was infamously small. The person followed up this info with a strangely malicious joke about how my mam's extra pounds (she was a few stone overweight) might bring the aircraft down. That was that. She began to spiral.

In spite of my dad's reassurances that there was no evidence that overweight people were bringing down flights, she begged him to cancel the trip. I heard the murmurings and tried to reason with her. I told her I'd mind her on the flight and that all the worry was just in her head. I pleaded with her to try to push through and that she'd be delighted with herself when she'd done it and was enjoying her holiday. But I knew that last bit was a lie. Even if she had managed to get on the plane, there'd have been some other issue over there – most likely my dad would have been flirting with another woman (no evidence); the hotel room would have been a health-and-safety deathtrap, etc. Anyway, she gave my pleas short shrift. The dream holiday was over.

We never did go to Jersey or take a family holiday. Mam changed and controlled the narrative: Dad didn't really want to go, he apparently was more of a home bird and happier having a few drinks in the local. He certainly didn't look happier to me. I didn't really want to go either, apparently. She told me that what I really wanted was a Sega Megadrive. This neutralised me. I'd never had a games console before except a second-hand Commodore 64 with an average game-loading time of around two weeks. She bought me off, masterfully. I shut up about Jersey. But I secretly wished that me and my dad had just gone on our own.

I was my mother's son, changing the world instead of myself when the need arose. Probably within the space of a few months, I had decided to hang up my Pioneer pin and join the ranks of the martyrs for drink. The pressure had become untenable. My radicalised teetotallers started a mutiny. One by one, they fell off the soft-drink wagon and brought back stories of wild abandon and, more importantly, girls. The word on the street was that you didn't need to overthink the kissing with a few drinks in you, it just seemed to happen. I'd lost control of them. I simply couldn't bear to be the odd man out. If you can't beat them, join them – and then beat them.

I remember it like it was yesterday. Junior Cert results night, out in the Lough, the sun dancing on the skin of the water of the lake on what that night certainly seemed to be a 'beautiful city, charming and pretty' – and this was my moment. I'd just lost the weight but I was wearing a massive green shirt. We weren't that poor – Mam could have afforded to get me a new shirt – I just liked the big one; it was almost like a memento of the bigger lad I used to be. I was like one of those guys on a

Slimfast diet, holding up the clothes they used to wear beside their brand-new selves, except I was still wearing them. But none of that mattered now, all that mattered was tonight. There would be gat (Corkish for alcohol). Who knew, there might even be ol' dolls (Corkish for girls). I brushed the gums off myself just in case and had a mouthful of blood as a result, like Cork's young answer to Bram Stoker's Dracula. Some duckin' and divin' past my dad was needed.

> Dad: Why are ya leaving so early?
> Me: Ah, ya know . . .
> Dad: Sure, you haven't even finished your dinner.
> Me: Ah, I'm just excited to meet my friends.
> Dad: You're not goin' drinkin', are ya?

Before I could even concoct some bullshit story, I saw him smiling at me, thinking, 'He's not goin' drinkin', he's a sap.' And I was a sap – happy to be one up until this point. The idea of going drinkin' and being more like my brothers? At this point? Terrifying. They were wild, fightin', hurlin', drinkin' folk. By comparison I was nerdy and nervy. But tonight was the night I thought I might just push through the terror.

So, I was sitting there in an alleyway in the Lough on the biggest night of my young life, in a way-too-big-for-me shirt and pants, brickin' it. I might be about to gat. Jesus Christ. *What if I do something weird like piss myself?* I thought. *What if I die? Oh God, what if I piss and shit myself?* I didn't have the guts to go to the off licence so it was up to B. B was the balls of the group. There was very little chat out of the rest of us as we waited, staring at the corner where we hoped he'd re-emerge. Our little heads were gone. You know when you're fifteen and you've got no real sense of how illegal your illegal activity is? You're assuming the worst. Was he going to get arrested? Shot? Lad buying cans for Junior Cert night? Hello! Helicopters! I could imagine this:

Pilot: Just surveying the scene here, captain. There's a young lad struggling up the road with a load of cans moving towards a young man in a giant green shirt. I repeat: giant, green. Over.

Captain: What's the thinking behind the giant green shirt, Steve? Over.

Pilot: Attempting to disguise himself as a shrub, Captain? For what dastardly end, we just don't— No wait, it's just a formerly fat kid with no sense of style!

But seemingly, against all odds, B dodged the helicopters. Coming around the corner, we saw a flash of red and white of the big, bulging offy bag o' cans. It was on. B was our shaman and the ceremony was about to begin. He conjured open a can for each of us – Scrumpy Jack. My heart felt like it was going to come out my mouth with the first appley assault on my tongue and the seductive aroma slithering up my nostrils. 'This is just Cidona with a little kick,' I said to myself. Jesus Christ, it was happening. I was trembling but it was quite nice and I was like, 'OK . . .' And I had another sip, and another, and it was grand! It was lovely. I felt light-headed straight away. *Oh my God, I'm doing it. I'm getting out of my head. Like my brothers, like the older lads in the estate, I'm drinking. I wish people could see me now. I'm gattin'!*

By the time I was halfway through my second can, I was standing on bollards, cracking jokes, the centre of the group, centre of the universe. Fast forward three cans and I was up on B's back, the giant green sail of my shirt flapping in the wind as we floated through the dusky skies of Barrack Street and landed in Sir Henry's nightclub. These oversized clothes were a boon now, if anything. I was a rapper, talking to girls, talking to lads, holding court, kissin', dancin', sneakin' in and out of toilets and suckin' down more cans because I was under no illusions – I was being fuelled here, I needed this stuff. Before I knew it my cans were gone. I found myself in the toilet with B. He left his by the sink when he was in the cubicle and instinctively I threw it down the hatch, didn't even think about it. As he was coming out, I feigned an altercation. Like, 'Hey, hey!' and told him some other lad just drank it. I wasn't known to lie – so he believed me. And we were off, tearing around the dance floor looking for the guy to teach him a lesson. Mad though, isn't it? Just lying straight away.

On the dance floor, I was carefree, bustin' moves. I was dire but I didn't give a shit. I was up on B's back again. We were bouncing off walls and gettin' drenched in other people's sweat but it was brilliant, it was extraordinary. I felt extraordinary.

I went into school the next morning and one of the lads turned around and went, 'Alright Tadhg, ya alcoholic,' and I was like, 'Oh boy!' Because back then, to our teenage brains, 'alcoholic' was a badge of honour. And I thought to myself, *This is it – I have my place. I have my cure for the 'something wrong, something not quite right'. This is who I am. I am the Gatman.*

I had ventured into Gatworld and it had gone spectacularly well. I never looked back. I had never felt so empowered in my life, because two things happened. One: the nervousness around girls, around socialising generally, about nightclubs, etc. was all taken care of with this magic potion. After just two or three cans, all the things that kept me up at night worrying seemed to evaporate. What a miracle drug. No wonder everyone in my childhood seemed to just be constantly on the piss! Life without alcohol immediately seemed unthinkable, which brings me to point two. Do you know that ol' squirmy feeling in the tummy I've been telling you about, the uncomfortableness, the gnawing fear? Gone. Without a trace. And without even the threat of returning long after the drink had left my system because I knew I was going back for more. I knew drink existed and what it could do; I now knew it was in the world with me and appeared to be the answer to every anxiety and discomfort I could imagine. As long as I had access to my equivalent of Popeye's spinach, the world was now my oyster and there would be plenty of Olive Oyls (Popeye's girlfriend. Apologies, a lot of my pop culture references are up to and over a hundred years old).

I'd be a boozehound. I'd come from good drink-sodden stock and all my idols were drunken writers, actors and musicians. But I was going to do it better. I was going to be a higher class of alcoholic entirely. No drinking cans at home and falling over with your head lodged up against the cooker for me. I was going to do a George Best (the early years) on it: parties, champagne and babes. Babes as far as the eye could see. Buckets and buckets of babes . . . or something. I was a deeply traumatised, delusional sixteen-year-old basket case who had just had his first four or five cans of Scrumpy Jack. And sitting in class the very first morning after the night before, there was nothing I could think of that could stop me.

And there really wasn't. It was Transition Year in school, effectively a year to pretend to your parents you're up to multifarious productive, valuable things when really, you're perfecting the means and methods of getting drunk as regularly and efficiently as little to no money would allow.

My friend S and I had a shared lust for the Doors and cheap cider, and, when we were being particularly brave, whiskey. We talked about how we were different to the other lads in school. After all, we had an appreciation for the great thinkers, such as Nietzsche (which I, at the time, went about merrily pronouncing as Nee-et-ski), William

Blake, James Joyce and a whole host of other people Jim Morrison had told us to like. We'd frolic on the Shakey Bridge in our own clothes with our school uniforms stuffed into gear bags and swap perspectives on books we hadn't read on a cocktail of Linden Village cider, whiskey and the egg sandwiches I was still somehow bringing to school. For years afterwards, every time I smelled egg, I'd smell whiskey and would briefly get excited before beginning to retch.

I'd loved Jim Morrison since I was a child. He was everything I was not. While still in primary school I'd sit in the front room of our house – cross-legged, my thighs nearly bursting out of the pants the next-door-neighbour made especially for me, with a bowl haircut and a face made for Clearasil – and engage in a staring competition with the image of him on the back of my sister's *An American Prayer* LP. Jim was lean, topless and beautiful, with his lips pursed and eyes going through ya for a shortcut. And yet in my fantastical mind, we'd so much in common. Difficulties with the mother, a godly singing voice, charming with the ladies and, most importantly, a desire for and fascination with getting wrecked. I read every book I could get my hands on, watched every documentary, listened to every bootleg tape. Imagine walking down the streets of Amsterdam with Grace Slick of Jefferson Airplane and taking every single drug that fans offered you on the street. Imagine being a sex god to women all over the world? Imagine having sex? Imagine writing a song about killing your father and canoodling with your mother. It was exciting, titillating and vicarious. At this stage, I'd barely talked to girls and though I was absolutely fascinated by them, I was terrified of drugs – and drink, for that matter, until my Scrumpy Jack initiation. My childhood fear of losing control of my mind and spiritual annihilation made me feel that, as much as I wanted to drink and drug, it could be too dicey a game to play. I was initially happy for Jim Morrison to do all the debauchery for me and I'd read about it in school under the desk during religion class.

Now I found myself attempting to adopt the Morrison doctrine as a guide for living rather than escapist fiction. I started to imagine myself as a Cork-south-central Lizard King. The first kiddie band I was in at school was called Far Arden (a quote from 'An American Prayer'). Our very first gig was in a city-centre pub called the Phoenix and I, the self-appointed lead singer who wasn't sure if he could sing yet, began by placing a giant mural of Jim Morrison's face at the back of the stage. I then slowly walked towards the microphone before absolutely butchering some rock 'n' roll classics while making mental notes about which Mount Mercy secondary-school girls were or were not falling for my parlour tricks. It's funny, if you completely commit to the persona, however ludicrous, it's amazing how many will go along with you for the ride. We all love a distraction.

Though I understood there was probably torturous pain lurking behind everything Morrison did, I didn't see myself in it. The last thing I wanted to do was assassinate my father – in any case, I was scared shitless of him and he'd have that gun out of my hand before I'd explained what was going on. And the actual very last thing I wanted to do was to have anything approaching a romantic exchange with my mam. I was fascinated by Morrison's death-drive but I didn't share it. But when my own drinking and drug-taking progressed, my world view started to change. I began to find myself on 'sessions' wanting to get more and more out of my head.

In S, I had found the (im)perfect partner in crime. S was a genuine wild child. He was taller and leaner than me, and, annoyingly, bore a closer resemblance to our spiritual leader, the ol' Lizard King. He waxed lyrical, as I did, about his contempt for authority. His intentions were to live outside the oppressive rules and norms of society. I was giving it all that but for me it was just talk. At sixteen and seventeen, I had the drinking under some sort of control and still harboured aspirations of getting a good Leaving Cert and doing 'well' – whatever that meant. I wanted to go to university. I wanted to have graduation ceremonies, get more pats on the back and make my family (particularly my dad) proud of me. But S meant what he said. Without a precedent amongst our peers, he left school and moved out of home at sixteen and dedicated himself to a hedonistic lifestyle. I was in awe. I was terrified by but also crazy attracted to the freedom and '*the road of excess leading to the palace of wisdom*' that he'd created for himself, and for now, that road was Barrack Street because it led from his crummy shared house to Sir Henry's nightclub, the rhythm and soul of the city's subculture.

One winter night, I called round after school and S offered me an Ecstasy tablet. I was confused. I thought Ecstasy was for brain-dead dance zombies. We were more refined, listening to complex rock 'n' roll, indie and jazz. I had assumed our drugs of choice would be weed and, if I plucked up the courage, acid.

S: No man, you don't get it. It's not so much about dancing. It's the way it makes you feel. You feel these waves of euphoria all over. It's like having a full-body orgasm for six hours straight.

That last sentence did nothing for me. A full-body six-hour orgasm sounded like carnage. I, believe it or not, hadn't started masturbating yet. To be fair, I had attempted it but, looking back, my technique was all over the place. I was treating the little chap like a joystick in a Commodore 64 fighting game, pulling it from side to side and occasionally button bashing the top. I'd feel a bit sore rather than sexually gratified in any way. So I decided to park the masturbation and just hold out for full human sex, which surely must be on the horizon, I reasoned. I would make sure I was good and drunk for it and feel absolutely nothing before, during and after: lovemaking Irish style. In the meantime, when the lack of masturbation created the irksome problem of nightly wet dreams, I would stuff some Dunnes Stores toilet paper down my jocks and get on with it, like a man.

So, while the orgasm bit bounced off me, the idea of waves of euphoria captivated my mind and stirred something in the depths of me. S and I were drinking Pernod and black. The plan was we'd have a couple more of these, take a Mitsubishi tablet each, wait for them to kick in (twenty-five minutes-ish) and then stroll into Henry's. I remember putting the tablet in my mouth, swallowing it back and thinking to myself, *This is all happening very fast*. What felt like a few weeks ago, I'd still been playing soccer on the street. Now, I was necking back class As and hanging out with people who were authentically anti-establishment. I was anti-establishment but still occasionally wanted to go to Mass and have people describe me as 'a nice young lad'.

I started to panic. I told S I wanted to go to the toilet and get sick, I was in over my head. I had double maths in the morning and I didn't have my homework done. I wanted to be a little boy again who wasn't railing against anything or constantly on the lookout for new and improved ways to get out of his head. S tried to calm me down and called in his new housemate Tony to reassure me. But Tony wasn't very reassuring-looking. He was handsome with penetrating blue eyes but clearly a fucking lunatic.

He came into the room in his dressing gown, visibly having been sampling the Mitsubishis all afternoon. He looked like the buzzed-up child of Bez from The Happy Mondays and the Dude from *The Big Lebowski*. He assured me there was nothing to worry about; I'd taken just one tablet; he'd taken ten and was, and I quote, 'grand'. Now, the man was far from grand. But it no longer mattered because as he remonstrated with me, I looked beyond his big, handsome, mad head to a poster on the wall of Che Guevara and this odd but gorgeous peace came over me. Though I admired the man greatly, the feeling had little to do with the Marxist revolutionary. The 'yoke' had started to kick in.

I floated outside. The cool, crisp December air was tasteable, like minty ice cream. Barrack Street, normally gritty enough to the eye, looked gay and merry like a scene from a winter Christmas village set. I glided among the happy road-dwellers who were slowly but surely being lured to the bottom of the street by the siren song of Henry's, riding waves of bliss, turning occasionally to S, saying things like, 'Are you feeling this?' In Sir Henry's, the music was good but irrelevant. I was more interested in people, in their heads, their energy, their kindness, the way their faces behaved when they were chatting and laughing. I had profound, meaty discussions in cubicles. I was interested in girls but without the tedious laddish-conquest mentality. I'd be more interested in painting a girl but I didn't go for it because (a) there were no paint and brushes in Henry's (there wasn't even soap) and (b) I was strictly a piss artist only.

Drink had made me feel like I always wanted to feel; Ecstasy was making me feel a way I hadn't even known was on offer. I almost couldn't take it. At one point, I sat on the ground in Sir Henry's (a notoriously dirty club) with human sweat seeping through the pores of the wall onto my head and just reflected on how beautiful and joyful the people dancing in the main room looked. A friend approached me. I knew him from the live music circuit. He was a well-meaning-enough fellow but a big fan of Metallica, which was a bit of a red flag in terms of a guy or girl being good craic. He said, 'Hey man, are you out of it?'

I said, 'I've never been more *in it*.'

He goes, 'What are ya at? Weed?'

I said, 'No, Ecstasy.' His face sharpened and his brow furrowed. He wagged a finger at me, slowly shook his head and walked away. I had apparently crossed the line and I was fuckin' loving it.

After the club, S and I walked the streets of Cork and I couldn't quite believe how beautiful the city was. Now, to be fair, I still feel like that sometimes when I'm walking around Cork and I haven't taken any yokes in years. We walked up by St Fin Barre's Cathedral, down by St Mary's of the Isle school and up the Lee, talking about how much we loved each other and our plans for the future, which involved low-key enough ambitions like leading Marxist revolutions, rock stardom and world peace.

I woke up the next morning, got myself together and went to school. I looked at my teachers, the lollipop lady, the other kids in my year, and I just felt sorry for them. There they were, living in a world that had yokes in it and none of them seemed to be taking them. They had no idea how happy they could be. Should I tell them?

Should I rent a truck and a loudspeaker and get as much of Cork City off their head as possible? Maybe. But first I needed to sample it many, many more times myself.

The following weekend, I'd another pill in my pocket cleverly wrapped in toilet roll (again with the Dunnes Stores toilet paper) in case anybody found it or I dropped it when looking for change. I was to meet S outside the off licence on Barrack Street but he was late. His phone was off, nothing unusual there. I said I might as well call down to the house. I strolled over there, barely able to contain myself with the excitement. Rat-a-tat-tat on his window and a large, aggressive-looking man in uniform answered the door and said, 'Who are you?'

'Anthony,' I said. Why on earth would I say that? Well, make sure you're sitting down – Tadhg is actually not my real name – at least, not on my birth certificate. My name is Anthony but shortly after I was born, my dad started calling me Tadhg because I somehow reminded him of his own father, Tadhg. Why I reminded my father of my notoriously tyrannical, obnoxious grandfather is neither here nor there. The point is this angry-looking man at the door was an authority figure and, as a reflex, I always gave my birth cert name when confronted with authority. On this occasion, that was a big mistake.

Tony was the guy they were looking for. Crazy, handsome Tony was suspected of banging out to half the south side of Cork and I had just wandered into a garda drug squad raid and inadvertently declared myself to be the wanted man. Next thing I knew, I was inside in S's room, pants around my ankles with a garda sticking his gloved hand up my ass to check for any illicit, lodged packages. To their surprise, the suspected drug-fuelled criminal only had one Ecstasy tablet, wrapped in bright orange Dunnes Stores toilet paper, on his person. Nonetheless, I was hauled down to the cop shop and sat in a room waiting for an interrogation.

To say I was in over my head was an understatement. I was barely past the stage of crying when I fell and hurt my knee, yet here I was in an episode of *Narcos*. I kept thinking about my dad. *If he finds out about this, I'm a dead man*. But more than that, he just wouldn't have understood the drugs thing at all and I was fearful he would be ashamed of me. That was unthinkable.

The DS garda ramped up my terror: 'First of all, you're a minor, so I'm going to have to tell your parents.'

Superb first play on his part. Not to be undone, I came back with a pretty robust move myself. I started crying and said, 'Please don't.'

He said, 'Tell me who you got the pill from and who's doing what in that house and I'll think about it.'

We were now in a battle of wits. I will infrequently pat myself on the back in these pages. There are few things more tedious in life than someone reflecting on their past and effectively coming to the conclusion that, 'I was kinda right about everything, actually.' I regularly make mistakes, I wreak havoc, but, at least in recent times, I have become aware of that and I try to make amends. I'm often the architect of my own misfortunes and regularly choose the wrong option but, sat there in the interrogation room with the DS lad licking his lips at the candy he was about to take from the frightened little baby in front of him, I'm kind of proud that I didn't wilt. 'I got it off a fella in a nightclub,' I said.

'You didn't.'

'I did, yeah.'

'I'm in this job about twenty years. Never once have I seen a drug dealer wrap something in orange toilet paper.'

'I think it's the new thing now.'

'What's your phone number, there? I'll give your folks a bell.'

'Ring my mam if you want but just to say her nerves are at her and I'd say it could finish her off.'

'Are you going to tell me the truth?'

'I bought it in a club and put toilet paper on it afterwards myself. Sorry I can't help ya, but I don't know anyone in the house except S and he's not a dealer, he's not a criminal, he's a good guy and he's my friend.'

Beat.

'Go on. Get out.'

I walked home and waited for the inevitable explosion at home. Would there be squad cars to the door? Would I be on *Crimecall*? Would we have to move house? Would my father hit the roof? Or at least use me to hit it? But that night passed, so did the next day and then a week. And for some reason, the DS never called. I got away with it. Lesson (not) learned.

Chapter Five

When the Great and Good Depart

So, I was sorted. I now had drink and drugs to combat the uncomfortableness within me and to help me access all the good things in life. I was on my way. And back then, I had a semblance of control. Even early on, I knew if I drank it would be a challenge not to go at it again the following day. So coming up to exams or important social engagements I simply wouldn't drink. I had to plan around my partying because I knew I was drinking differently to my friends. I was aware my relationship with the stuff was madder and deeper. But I was still doing well in school and even though Mam's falls and general madness were worse than ever, I didn't seem to care as much. I was on my own journey now.

I also seemed to have gone from zero to hero with the ladies. In the spirit of digging deep and unearthing some ugly truths, I had an extremely unhealthy outlook on women at the time. It is not an excuse but more of an explanation: when you're repeatedly hurt by the most important female in your life and you're also spurned as the fat boy, you tend to treat new-found attention from girls with cynicism.

At that first kiddies' band gig in the Phoenix, I caught the eye of M smiling up at me. M went to our sister school and was known as the top tottie. All the lads fancied her but, cocky as I was, I was quick to dismiss the smiling. I was more focused on ploughing through my gig, smoking the spliff in my bag I'd pre-prepared and then getting blind drunk. But after the gig, her friend walked up to me and told me M liked me. I remember the friend telling me with a quizzical look on her face. She clearly didn't see whatever M was seeing. But what *was* M seeing?

Back at an after-party that night we talked and kissed and made some plans to go on a date, and I got horribly drunk to take the edge off the feelings, good an' all as they were. Drink had a gorgeous way of just dialling down reality to a more manageable level. That night was amazing. M was beautiful, kind and smart. In my drunken, immature head, I found the envious glances of other lads almost the best part of the experience. And when they were starting to repeat themselves or get sick in the garden or order cabs home, I was staying on with the girl. After that night we began going out with each other. Nothing could stop me now.

Except, of course, for fear. I'd flown too high, too quickly. I couldn't sustain it, I told myself. I couldn't comfortably believe that M liked me or that I was the envy of the other lads. M would see through me pretty quickly, I thought. Realise I wasn't as smart as I pretended to be, not as good-looking, that I didn't wear the right clothes, didn't have the brands, that I got handouts from school to buy books and uniform, and was growing up in relative poverty while a lot of the people I mixed with seemed to be living in Barry's Tea adverts, where houses looked orderly and cosy and everyone seemed happy to be with each other. This was unsustainable.

I started to withdraw. I'd leave her texts unanswered. I'd speak about the girl disrespectfully or indifferently to friends. When we were together at parties, I'd half avoid her. I acted like someone who could take or leave the relationship, whereas in actual fact, I was mad about her. I just felt that, at any moment, she'd find out who I really was and dump me and then everyone, including me, would know the truth: I wasn't good enough.

At a party one night, I began flirting with one of her friends and expressed my undying love for her. My angle was that we'd be free to run off together when I got rid of the ball and chain. Word got out and M confronted me. I pleaded my innocence and blamed the friend. I was a coward as well as a little shit. I couldn't face the conflict I was constantly creating. M initially took my side but about a week later, another one of her friends saw me kissing someone else in Sir Henry's (there really was just one good nightclub in Cork). The jig was up. M cut me loose. What a relief.

I felt more comfortable now that it was over and I could spin the narrative to the lads that I got caught cheating and she couldn't handle it. Wow, this guy is so cool. He gets the hottest girl in school and treats her like

shit. What a legend. I hoped that's what they were thinking, anyway. But it just wouldn't be accurate to say that
I dwelt on these things too much at that age. I knew I had
damage; I knew I was treating people badly, especially
myself at times, but I didn't care, certainly not enough
to make any changes. Having discovered the elixir that
made me Gatman, I was young, free and wild, flying
through the skies of Cork City, engaged in the eternal
battle of good-and-drunk versus evil. Going from house
parties to nightclubs to house parties to school to girlfriends' houses, where their mams were the opposite of
mine, smelling of perfume and doing wonderous regular-
Irish-mam things, like pulling a delicious Sunday roast
out of the oven. I was going to get a good Leaving Cert;
I was going to university; I was going to take it handy
on the booze when I needed to. I was going to get myself
away from my mother at my earliest opportunity and I
was going to grab life by the bullhorns and kiss her on
the mouth. I was happy as a pig in shit.

And then my dad died.

On Saturday, 16 December 2000 I was getting ready
to go out. Getting ready, for this eighteen-year-old,
amounted to wiping sleep out of my eyes, brushing my
teeth, putting on the brown leather jacket I had commandeered from my sister and running out the door. On
this particular night, I was going to a concert in Cork
Opera House. My sister and her partner would be there
too. We were going to see Jack L, who both me and my

sister adored. We'd seen him together before. Never in my life had I heard such a pure celestial voice, and I'd certainly never seen somebody gyrate with a red feather boa to a largely terrified group of onlookers in Mitchelstown main square. At one stage during that gig, he'd looked over in our general direction and me and my sister turned to each other and each claimed he was singing 'Rooftop Lullaby' directly to us. We'd flamboyant, playful egos, me and sis, as did Jack L. We were all just perfect for one another.

My loose plan was to get mildly drunk before the concert, go and find a party afterwards, and come home at all hours, as was becoming my pattern. Before I ran out the door, my dad stopped me. 'Come home early tonight now and don't be worrying your mother again.' My mother, by now a nervous wreck, self-medicating with alcohol, was being pushed towards her wits' end by my staying out all night, and he was undoubtedly getting the brunt of her grisly predictions about what was ultimately going to happen to me. But his voice was more earnest than stern. He was trying to be reasonable and I answered affirmatively in a reassuring tone. But as I walked down the road, I thought to myself, *Does he really mean that? He's getting on a bit now. He's probably not going to hit me or properly snap anymore.* I still had the utmost respect for him and, I would say, a healthy fear, but I already knew that when I picked up it was very difficult to know when I'd put it down again. I had a bit of a battle in my head: *He doesn't ask you to do much. You've literally just said to his face you'll be back. Just come home after the concert, your Christmas exams are starting Monday anyway. Get a grip, you're not Keith Moon.*

The concert was pure magic. I was still at that age when even just being out at night in pubs and clubs was cool. I felt like a proper grown-up – no drinkin' cider in parks or alleyways for me anymore. I was necking my plastic-cup pints, chatting to old people (thirty+) and everything. This was momentous. Me and my girlfriend at the time, my sister, her partner and their friends had a ball and sang all the words to 'Georgie Boy', 'Rooftop Lullaby' and 'When the Moon Is High'. I floated out of the Opera House and have vague memories of drinking in the Spailpín Fánach with some randomers. I wouldn't have been keeping an eye on the time but when you've lost your girlfriend and sister and find yourself back at a party in an unknown location hours after you've left the gig, you know it's probably late. You know your promise of coming home early and not worrying your mam has been compromised.

I don't remember how or when I got home. I woke up to the phone ringing. I heard my mother answering it in the living room, which meant she was up, which meant my dad had already left to go fishing, as he regularly did on Sundays. Her voice sounded panicked and she called my sister downstairs to talk to the person on the phone. My sister's voice amplified the panic so I ran down. The call was from my father's friend. My

81

dad had fallen over and was on the way to hospital but we weren't to worry. We all worried. As we were getting ready to go to the hospital, the phone rang again. It was the friend again, this time saying that in fact the situation wasn't looking good. Why this usually straight-talking man was flip-flopping and conversing in code I wasn't sure. Now, I realise that the poor man was probably just shocked himself. My dad was a person whom you somehow thought was unlikely to die. Perhaps my dad's mate rightly worried that my mother wouldn't be able to endure the news.

I felt my world imploding. And so I did what I always did in a crisis – when I'd taken too many drugs and I felt sure I was about to lose my mind, when I'd kissed someone else's girlfriend and the lad was about to kick the shit out of me, when a loved one was in peril – I ran upstairs into my parents' bedroom, dropped to my knees and eyeballed the picture of the Sacred Heart, which sat on the wall facing their bed. It was one of those ancient, creepy ones with the red light in front of himself. 'Please don't let him die. I'll never stay out late again, I'll never take drugs again, I'll join the priesthood. I'll do whatever you want me to do, just please don't let him die.' I couldn't even get to a second round of the prayer. I knew he was gone.

We packed into my sister's Fiesta in a daze. Christmas was looming and I remember 'Silent Night' playing on the radio during the short drive to the hospital. We piled into the room he was in. I put my hand on his face and his baldy head. He looked quite regal lying there. There was no anguish or distress on his face and I remember thinking, *If today is his last day, what a massive impact he's made on the world, on me, on all of us.* But I was also terrified. He was the glue that kept this raggle-taggle band of misfits together. What was going to happen to us now?

We were ushered into a family room and a bespectacled doctor informed us that our father had 'expired'. Expired? I resented that word for years afterwards. I'm not sure if it's the official, medical term that you're supposed to give an inconsolable family or he was just a prick but I would have thought 'expired' is a more fitting description of some mouldy cheese at the back of the fridge, rather than how you tell someone their whole world has come apart. Even though I was always conscious that my dad was a bit older than my friends' dads, he still was only in his mid-sixties and was as strong as on ox. He was infinitely healthier than my mam and it was hard to accept he was gone. I was eighteen. It was Christmas of my Leaving Cert year. I wasn't ready.

The rest of the afternoon was a bit of a blur. I remember hugging my brother Alan. We were always close but I don't ever remember hugging him before. I remember my mother wailing that she couldn't cope, that she wouldn't be going to the funeral, that she'd be better off dead herself now. She was drunk and maudlin, and in those moments, when she somehow made the occasion of my father's death all about her, I wished it had been her and not him who'd pissed off. I would have given anything. But I was also disgusted with myself, ashamed. The very last thing my wonderful father would ever ask of me, and I let him down. There was something about the finality of that, the inability to undo it, that overwhelmed me. If he thought about me when fishing that morning, what went through his head? Did he go to meet his maker with anger in his heart for me, or worse still, disappointment? But those feelings were powerful and poisonous and I needed them to stop.

As the day progressed, something familiar that had served me well throughout childhood kicked in: dissociation – I'm not here, this isn't happening. I accepted I'd been to a hospital and had been told that my father was dead but what I was in denial about was that this was anything to get worked up about. I felt like if I faced up to the enormity of it right then, I'd go under. So my brain just seemed to go, 'Nah'. Brains are brilliant, in fairness. Shock, denial, whatever you want to call it, was a very welcome addition to the experience.

I walked out the Lough in the pissing rain and called round to my friend B's house. He let me into his front room.

B: Are you alright? You look kinda mental.

Me: Mental? How?

B: Well, you've no coat on and you're soaking wet. And your eyes look kind of weird.

Me: Nah, I'm grand, boy. How did ye get on last night?

B: Same ol' shit. Maltings and then Club FX. Club FX was brutal. You?

Me: Was at the Jack L gig. Unreal. My dad died this morning, alright though.

B: What?

Me: Ya, my dad died this morning. Look, these things happen.

I really feel for B, looking back on it: seventeen years old, previous experience in traumatic events pretty much just the night his fake ID was stolen in the Maltings and he couldn't go out for two weeks while he waited for the new one, and yet here he was, confronted by a drenched lad fit for a psych ward. Next thing I remember is being in a different room of the house talking to B's dad, L.

L: What happened your dad, Tadhg?

Me: He got a heart attack and died.

L: I'm truly sorry to hear that, my man.

Me: Ah, thanks buddy.

I honestly didn't fully grasp why he had tears in his eyes and just stood there regarding me. Because I felt numb. After a few moments of silence, he put his arms around me and told me everything was going to be OK. That was nice. I liked that. We had been pretty close before this but a bond began with that hug that persists today.

I was very moved by the fact that my whole year attended the funeral. The day before, my English teacher,

Mr O'K, had knocked at my door to offer condolences and leave me a card and a poem by Wordsworth:

> *But when the great and good depart*
> *What is it more than this –*
> *That man, who is from God sent forth,*
> *Doth yet again to God return?*
> *Such ebb and flow must ever be;*
> *Wherefore shall we mourn?*

I absolutely adored Mr O'K. Me and him had a bit of a *Dead Poets Society* mutual-admiration thing going on, but his consideration for me, his humanity, his empathy stunned me.

I loved my father dearly, almost obsessively. No, definitely obsessively. His passing should have been an occasion for deep grief and loss. But many years of putting on a front and/or the shock and denial kept me quite detached from mourning. I cried when I felt the gaze of my school friends on me in the graveyard. I wore black like Hamlet and started to become quite proficient at the grieving-young-son interactions with neighbours. But all of it was tainted with just a little bit of artifice. I was playing the role of an almost mortally wounded mourner, as well as actually being one at the same time. And the performative aspect of my grief had a clear utility in my mind: I was going to get away with murder now. *My mother is an alcoholic basket case and I've lost my guide, my source of strength, my superhero. This will now translate into a free pass to do as I like, indefinitely.* The world, it seemed, was consistently dealing me cruel hands, which was completely unfair because I was a really, really nice guy who was just trying to bring joy to Cork city centre and suburbs.

However, for the next few months, I reined myself in somewhat. I'd a Leaving Cert to do and, in spite of the encroaching recklessness, I still had my pride. In the end, I did very well and received the now-familiar plaudits from teachers, that went something like, 'Fair play to him for doing as well he did, considering . . .' They were, of course, referring to my father's passing. But now, living with a nihilistic mother was in many ways much more difficult and painful than the bereavement. Her drinking and death drive became more extreme. Her self-care went out the window and without my sister and later, her incredible home helps, it would have stayed there. In drunken sincerity, she'd reiterate her desire to also be dead now that my dad was gone. I think I was so nervous that she was going to drink herself to death or fall and knock herself out that I curtailed my own drinking and drug-taking for a few months. But after the Leaving Cert and in the build-up to going to college, I went to the other extreme. This was to become a pattern. For weeks, sometimes months at a time, I'd be the model son: 'What a great lad, looking after his poor mam.' And then for days and weeks the drinking and drug-taking would be out of all control. I'd be climbing in the toilet window at all hours, behaving like somebody who was actively trying to finish off his mother's nerves. After much soul-searching, I don't believe that's what was going on, though. I was just trying to deal with my own pain. And drink and drugs were unbelievably effective anaesthetics.

There was certainly an aspect to the partying that was different for a while after my dad died. It was angrier. It was excessive beyond the point of fun. I remember one night drinking whiskey and taking Valium and falling asleep on the road, then waking up on the footpath and heading off to a party to take Ecstasy. I knew that mixing all those substances together was dangerous but I was starting to seek something beyond feeling good. It was more than painlessness: I'd developed a hankering for oblivion. At the party I snapped, broke down in tears and poured my heart out about my dad's death to strangers, presumably weirding everyone out.

Meanwhile, Mam was slowly driving me and my sister insane, and I wanted to be out of my head as often as my part-time night-packing job in Roches Stores would allow. I was now identifying with the Jim Morrison drink-and-drug ethic in a way that I didn't want to. It wasn't all that much fun in this period. I put it down to grief and yet deep down inside, I knew I hadn't even processed my father's death. I was unwilling to even consider that the drink and drugs weren't working as well as they had been. So, I decided my best bet was to take more, hit it harder and hopefully break through the rough patch.

Chapter Six

A Snowball's Chance in Hell

By August 2003 I was twenty and out of control. There was a new drug going around the country we called 'Snowballs'. It was some sort of fusion of Ecstasy, LSD and speed. The trip lasted at least twenty-four hours and was meant to be the most mental and intense experience imaginable. Up the country, some poor lad had gouged his eyes out thinking there were rats running around his head. A few friends of mine had taken it the weekend earlier: one hadn't left the house since and the other was looking and acting like somebody who had just come back from the Somme. I thought to myself, *I'll have a bit of that.*

Very few were up for it, for some reason. I knew I could at least always count on D. D was my most trusted, dedicated and enthusiastic booze buddy from the start right up until endgame. I think we probably would have done anything for each other and we often did. It's why I always shy away from the idea that some people have that when you go into recovery you need to regard your drinking buddies as universally disingenuous and uncaring. I had a few, perhaps not many, so-called 'drinking buddies' that I still call friends today. It's not a black-and-white thing. Nothing is. You could be using somebody as a foil, an excuse, an enabler for your addiction and still love them very much. I believe you're capable of love even when in the heights of addiction. Love alone just can't get you sober. That's my experience, anyway.

So D and I were in a superb Cork bar called Sin É and I sent a text to our man in Columbia, i.e. Ballyphehane, to sort us out. In my head, I was the man. Friends who were not up for snowballs were weak in my eyes. I thought to myself, *Look at all the shit going on in my life. You don't see me moping about the house, derailed by a night on the sesh. Middle-class cowards.*

We booked a cab and before we left to go back to D's house via Ballyphehane to start the day-long trip, I got chatting to this old lad up at the bar and filled him in on my plan for the evening. He said he used to smoke a bit of weed but he hadn't done any acid for twenty years. I said, 'You're more than welcome, there's plenty to go round.' In my head now I'm fuckin' Pablo Escobar, a lynchpin of the Cork drug scene but a good guy with it, buying football pitches for the kids and whatnot, bringing auld lads on nostalgic acid trips.

So me, D, a couple of the other lads and this auld fella zoom off to D's via Ballyphehane, laughing our heads off. In the cab on the way back to D's, D attempts to convey, in the most poorly executed coded speech

I'd ever heard in my life, that it would be best not to take the drugs in the cab in case we come up off them. I just told him to whisht up, mostly because I'd already taken mine.

The first few hours were magnificent. It just felt like slightly more intense Ecstasy than I was used to, with hallucinogenic embroidery to sound and vision, and the spiritual connectedness that one associates with a positive acid experience. Me and the auld lad were out in D's garden in the early hours, staring into the sky, speechless at the beauty of the breaking day, having a Blakean vision as the painterly hands of God touched up the landscape for our benefit. Tears came to my eyes. Me and this *auld lad* were just two travellers on this earth trying our best, I thought, being inconspicuously minded by a benevolent, ever-compassionate creator who no doubt would await us when we had completed our journeys, as we transcended these eye-watering skies into the artist's studio itself. We drank, we listened to music and I was overcome with the feeling that everything was going to be alright.

There were two lads I didn't know at the party: one tall with shaggy hair and his smaller, more rotund chum. They appeared to be metal fans, the proper, geeky variety. As I mentioned before, I usually go out of my way to avoid metal fans but in this blissful state of consciousness I took it upon myself to not only get to know them but to love and cherish them. To bring them outside to see God in the garden.

After a few hours, things took a turn. It was almost as if someone else was going at the painting and all his additions made it ugly, frightening. Reality was still embellished; it just wasn't enjoyable anymore. The *auld lad* and the two weird metallers now looked to me more like Ted, Dougal and Mrs Doyle look to Father Jack after he drinks the Toilet Duck. But there was no laughter track. I started to feel like I was quietly going insane. I tried engaging in conversations with D or someone else or drinking cans or listening to music or watching two other lads who seemed to have a way better handle on things than I did, playing FIFA, but these were mere interstitials. There seemed to be no stopping the procession to madness.

Acid and mushrooms have a way of tapping into your secret, dormant fears and phobias and punching you in the head with them, kicking you in the stomach, which often brings about a therapeutic, cathartic effect. But this was different. This didn't feel like beneficial suffering. My deepest terrors were all on the surface; I could feel them on my skin. I was simply terrified of going mad. Of my brain bursting with the tension. I was still that kid in the toilet, telling Mam that my head felt too hot to do my homework, visualising ambulances being called to the door, humiliating my friends and family, bringing shame to the house. I'd snapped.

I silently prayed for it to end. It had to end. I announced to the room, 'Amazing stuff but you'd be kind of getting sick of it after a while, wouldn't ya? Looking forward to the end?' One of the lads in the group, a charismatic little eccentric from the north side of the city replied, 'I don't think this will ever end,' and he lay back on the couch laughing. As he did, I felt as if steel shutters had come crashing down around my mind and I was now permanently locked inside it. I learned afterwards that the same fella, coming to the end of his trip, just popped another one straight away and must have gone through the whole terrifying process all over again. Years later, that bright star was extinguished. When he died, I couldn't help thinking about that night and imagining and empathising with the pain and trauma he must have been trying to distract himself from on the 'sesh'. And how drink and drugs carry all your pain for a while and then one day turn on you and fuck the whole lot of it on top of you until you can't breathe.

I left D's house about sixteen hours after popping the pill, still absolutely out of my mind. I decided to walk the few miles to B's house (the lad who had to deal with me after my dad died) in some sort of an attempt to walk off the insanity, as if it were cramp. But unfortunately, by the time I got to the Lough, the mad-cramp had only gotten worse. B let me in reluctantly – his folks were out. He gave me some more gat from the drinks cabinet. I felt like I'd been drinking solidly for twenty-four hours now; how there was no sleepiness or tipsiness was in equal measures baffling and horrifying. He let me lie down on his bed to see if I could somehow get some rest. I'd an hour or two's grace before his parents would come back and I set my alarm. I lay down and tried to think happy thoughts but got back up about thirty seconds later because I kept imagining myself jumping out the bedroom window. I went downstairs, said, 'Thanks for the nap,' and shuffled out the door.

I began doing looney loops of the Lough, darting in and out of the never-more-menacing-looking geese and swans. It's hard to put this kind of frenetic madness into words. I wasn't really hallucinating anymore. I wasn't hearing voices. I wasn't thinking about hurting other people, I was just in the midst of a full-body panic attack that showed no signs of abating. And the thoughts. Fucking hell. *You're mad now. This is the end; you've fucked your brain. You're never getting out of it. Kill yourself.* They played on an endless loop backed up, reinforced by the feelings.

Worn out from walking and dodging glances from the odd neighbour, I threw in the towel and walked the few minutes back to the family home, gambling that my mam would be drunk and wouldn't pick up on my erratic behaviour. Then I could talk to my sister if she was in. I felt like I'd been awake for about ten years, forced to watch a horror film about my own demise on a loop, like Alex DeLarge in *A Clockwork Orange.*

My sister, to her eternal credit, always had this marvellous way of disguising her own fear when I presented myself to her in drink- and drug-fuelled distress. She listened to my incoherent rambling that must have gone something like: 'I've taken this superdrug, at the start it was great, I was chatting to God and whatnot but for around the last sixteen hours it's telling me I'm probably going to have to be put into a psychiatric unit because I'm brain-damaged and I just really need to sleep.' She calmly went to the kitchen, got me some of my mam's Valium and gently ushered me upstairs with a cup of water. I took two or three D10s and thought to myself, *What chance do these little blue fuckers have when a bottle of brandy and about fifteen cans couldn't land a punch?* But as I lay there thinking that, I noticed that my brain was ever so slightly quietening down. The tightness in my chest was easing a little, as were the vice grips in my stomach. I thought to myself, *I might as well take another couple of them.* And off I went to nighty-nighty snoozy-woozy land, and there I lived happily till about two o'clock the next day.

When I woke I felt reasonably OK, which in the context of the previous day was amazing. I was looking out the window, like Scrooge post-epiphany: 'You there, boy. What day is it?' 'It's You-don't-have-to-go-to-a-locked-ward day, Sir.' I felt like dancing and singing and an eternal truth about myself became clear there and then. In spite of the pain that had been and the undoubted pain that was to come, I loved life. I loved being alive. I don't think I ever fully lost gratitude for the ordinary magic of being on this planet, able to roam around relatively freely chatting to my mates, cracking jokes, falling in love, being blown away by great art. And it is a tragedy that many people who end up being overwhelmed by their problems, or at least their thoughts and feelings, probably felt the same way I did at some point. They didn't want to die; they just wanted the pain to stop.

Sadly, the resurrection was short-lived. Over the next few days, I felt like I was slipping in and out of the bad trip again. I was having these quite disturbing emotional flashbacks. The following weekend, I still felt ropey. I thought my best bet now was just to get drunk. I drank all Friday night and when I woke up Saturday morning, I felt bizarre – ring-the-doctor bizarre. But I brushed it off again (some man for the brushing off) and went to Douglas Court Shopping Centre to meet my partner at the time. At some point in the afternoon she was talking but I couldn't hear what she was saying and my head felt like it was on fire again. I made my excuses and went to the toilet. My heart was pounding and I felt as bad or worse as when I had been looping the Lough. I had somehow become aware at this point that it was a panic attack and I knew they ended so I thought maybe I just need to ride it out. But it was harder than I had imagined and all I kept thinking was: I need a drink, I need a drink.

I got back into the city and had a few pints with the lads, somehow managing to take it handy because I was trying to find the magic number of drinks that would take the edge off this thing without making it worse. But on Sunday morning I woke up and the panic was still there. Cork and Wexford were playing in the All-Ireland hurling semi-final and me and a few mates were heading up to Dublin, which meant that I had free rein to drink all day and night without anyone batting an eyelid. But the raw terror during the journey was debilitating. I felt I was going to open the door of the car and hurl myself into a ditch. I kept thinking, *Just open the door and do it.* Over and over. I slurped down bottles of beer with trembling hands, now with no choice but to get wasted.

It didn't make much of a dent in the panic and when I woke up Monday morning, it was at a ten and I was hysterical. I pretty much ran to the doctors and explained everything that had happened. Before this I'd only ever see the man once in the blue moon for a chest infection or the like. We'd chat about music and he'd send me on my way. I used to imagine myself as a delightful palette cleanser between his other, no doubt boring and demanding, patients. If he was rattled by my fit-for-hospitalisation demeanour, he didn't show it. He told me firstly that there was nothing to worry about because people who think they're going insane are actually sane. You'd only be going insane if you thought you were grand. Whether that's true or not, it was a massive comfort at the time. And two – and to be fair to him he was quite correct here – the panic attacks and flashbacks I was experiencing were very common after acid experiences. I said, 'Doc, it wasn't just acid though, it was snowballs. It's like acid 2.0 and it's after blowing my brain apart.'

He said, 'Look, I think your brain is intact. I assure you it's anxiety. Medication is an option but I don't think we're going to go there yet. See how you go over the next few days.'

It's funny. In this whole period I don't ever remember connecting the terror in my mind to the chaos going on at home with my mam or the death of my father just two years earlier. I was entirely focused on the idea that I'd destroyed my brain with too many drugs and I was now a full-on lunatic, whispering to himself to jump out doors and windows. Had I taken a little bit less, I'd probably still be at the party, happy out. I thought endlessly about rewinding and not taking that fucking snowball. I could see no way back to 'normality'. My brain felt different, damaged. My next repetitive thought was, *Maybe I'm having a brain haemorrhage.* Before long, I was back at the doctor and we talked about my drug use in more depth. The snowballs incident wasn't an isolated event; I'd been taking Ecstasy in large quantities pretty much every weekend for the previous couple of years and drinking to oblivion on top of it. The doctor said my serotonin was probably depleted.

'Can you take a tablet for that?' I asked.

'Yes and they're very effective,' he replied.

Oh boy! I thought to myself. *Hold on a second now, this is extraordinary news! You can go out, batter yourself with drink and drugs till you're shivering in the corner absolutely out of your box in existential terror and then you can just take a pill and you're right as rain? Well thank you big pharma. You've done it again!*

Sure enough, after about four-and-a-half to five days on 10mg of Lexapro, I went from hopeless and terrified to a lad who felt like he was on a mild but beautiful everlasting yoke-stopper. It was unbelievable. I could drink away again grand – albeit with sporadic incidents of bed-wetting and irrational violence. I could take Ecstasy again guilt free, including proudly taking twenty-one yokes the night of my twenty-first birthday for a dare. I barely got anything off them but I also barely felt any repercussions the next day. The Lexapro had somehow raised my base level of mental well-being: an addict's dream. Just as well, 'cause I'd a few things to do over the next couple of months.

The first of which was to make my Edinburgh Fringe Festival debut.

When I was drinking, I always found the depictions of alcoholism on TV and film relentlessly bleak. You'd generally have a scene with a lad sitting in his underpants crying and throwing an empty bottle of whiskey at a picture of his deceased wife. But the truth of the matter is that I know very few alcoholics who didn't have an absolute hoot on their way to eventual despair. We wouldn't be so preoccupied with drinking if it weren't absolutely brilliant. And I do think it's important to say that because I've always found the best way you can help someone struggling with addiction is to be honest with them. If you come in hot with the 'drink and drugs are evil' routine, you run the risk of alienating them. Drink and drugs are superb until they stop working.

For me, certainly, there were periods when I wasn't drinking to alleviate depression or trauma. I was just drinking because it was unbelievable craic and I was very good at it. I think every drinker has a little spell in their life, often linked to a place or time, that they see as the highlight, the party peak. And really thereafter you're just chasing it, trying to engineer an approximation of that high. Edinburgh 2002 was that for me. It was my first real trip away from home, away from the octopusian (if that's not a word then it should be) clutches of Mam; my daughter hadn't arrived on the scene yet – of which more, later – and I was also on an ego trip. In spite of not being particularly interested in becoming an actor (in college I was in and out of various bands pursuing the Jim Morrison 2.0 dream) only having one show on my acting CV and that a college production of *Jesus Christ Superstar*, I'd bizarrely been headhunted by Classik Attak to do one of only two funded plays from Cork travelling to the prestigious Fringe Festival. It was a two-hander called *Judas*, written and directed by Helen Kavanagh-Ronan, and I would be playing the titular character. Imagine having an ego of biblical proportions and Jesus and Judas are your first two acting roles. What a guy. What a range. I thought I was Robert de Niro just after booking the *Taxi Driver* gig.

Still, I remember me and my sister holding each other in Cork airport before I got on the plane, both bawling our eyes out. Anybody looking at us must have assumed that I was emigrating as opposed to going to an arts festival for a few weeks. Such was the level of dysfunction at home. I arrived in Edinburgh worn out from crying with visceral guilt as to what was in store for my sister back home. Looking back on it now, it's hardly much of a surprise that Edinburgh was as insane as it was.

Initially, I'd no plans to go boozing – well, at least, not chaotically. I was there primarily to do a job. I was travelling alone anyway. The director of the play and the other actor were already there and so I'd probably just keep myself to myself in the hostel, have a few drinks after the odd show, soak up the atmosphere in the festival and go home.

What actually happened was a two-month drink-and-drug marathon with occasional outbreaks of theatre. Day one in the youth hostel I was on my own in the TV room, channel hopping late at night, when two balmpot Dublin young ones came in after a night on the tiles. After about a three-to-four-minute conversation we were friends for life and burst open a few cans. M suggested we go for a pint.

'It's five o'clock in the morning, girl.'

'Yeah, the early house in Leith has just opened.'

I couldn't believe it. I hadn't been to the morning pubs in Cork yet but I had heard they were magical places to be, where day was night and night was day, where the thinkers were drinkers and the thoughts always merry. A veritable Wonka factory for booze hounds. But nothing could have fully prepared me for the sights and sounds, the majesty that awaited me behind the doors of that pub in Leith that morning: a 5 am sing-song in full swing; a bored but good-humoured young Irish barmaid behind the counter; jovial albeit virtually impossible-to-understand older Scottish men and women asking me where I was from and what I was drinking. As far as I was concerned, the play I'd come over to Edinburgh to perform became an irrelevance. This was the real show and I was the lead.

There were times when I had to ring in sick for the performance. In my head, it was as if I were ringing in to my night-packing job in the supermarket, not to a show at a major festival where technicians, a director, an ambitious, irate co-star, reviewers and, of course, an audience were depending on me not drinking or taking drugs earlier in the day. The director, Helen, was living in the same accommodation as I was. She was dumbfounded to bump into me the morning after the night I'd called in sick, returning from the local off licence with a case of wine in each hand and two plastic bags for shoes (I'd lost them in some no-doubt-hilarious high-jinks escapade).

Other days I'd turn up so spaced out and sleepy after being up all night taking Ecstasy that I'd just mumble my way through the play and react several beats after I should have done. The other actor was a robust Australian, eager to put himself in the shop window for TV and film work with international producers, and he let his frustration with my lacklustre commitment spill over on stage one night when a theatrical brawl between the two characters became so real that I woke up the next morning with bruises all over my chest and back. This was probably my first visceral impression at how frustrating it was to deal with me when I was off on one. But at this stage I was really just having too much of a good time to really care.

I also hit it off with this large Tipperary lad in the hostel who had that same wanton eye for mayhem as myself. The two of us were built for chaos. He was working with a street vendor, a large flamboyant geezer from Manchester. Together they sold built-to-break toys on Princes Street but were rarely available for buyer's remorse. I fell out of the early house in Leith one morning and was stumbling home when Tipp and the geezer got out of a taxi. Geezer looked at me. I'd long hair at the time, God love me, with blonde streaks in it, the trademark Jim Morrison T-shirt and the sister's brown leather jacket.

Geezer: Are you gay?
Me (nervously): No.
Geezer: Well, you're no good to me then.

The three of us instantly hit it off. Geezer announced he'd love a bit of crack cocaine to wind down but didn't know anyone in Edinburgh who supplied it. I attempted to empathise with his crack-lack frustration but secretly I was really scared – this was levelling up from Ecstasy big time. Not to mention I had a show that night with an angry Aussie liable to kick my head in. But I wanted my new lunatic Madchester buddy to think I was cool, so before we knew it, we were getting a train to Glasgow to go to a caravan park to smoke crack for the morning. On the way, I said to Geezer, 'Would you be able to do a play after crack?'

He said, 'Is it an introspective play?'

I said, 'It is a bit, ya.'

'Smoke your brains out, so,' he said.

I lay on my back on the caravan floor. Me and Tipp looked at each other, I'm sure thinking: *I wonder, is it too late to ring our mams?* But also thinking, *Holy shit, we're about to smoke crack like in the movies. Wait till the guys and girls in the hostel hear this!* I fumbled a little with the empty can, the rock and the lighter, but after a couple of false dawns it hit me and I felt like I was melting into the ground. There was this weird, paradoxical feeling of being more aware than ever that I was consuming a substance in a crummy caravan, obviously trying to contrive a buzz in the least natural way imaginable, and yet the feeling itself was the most natural, joyful and peaceful I'd ever experienced. Almost enlightened. But what didn't suit me about it was that this feeling doesn't really last, and then you find yourself on your hands and knees on a caravan floor with a six-foot-four-inch country boy from Tipp and a three-hundred-pound geezer looking for bits of rock you may have accidentally dropped.

I don't remember much more. I know I slept and I remember getting the train back to Edinburgh with Tipp and us proud as Punch, talking about the people in our lives and who would or would not have the balls to try what we described as 'the big two': crack and heroin. It was all just a game, back then. We hadn't a clue what we were talking about. I'd cringe when I recalled these . . . recall those conversations and thoughts. I had no grasp at all of the seriousness of the situations I'd been in. Had crack been available in Cork at that time, I don't know where I would have been because I thought about the high of it every day for weeks afterwards. I don't cringe anymore, though. I now have a bit of empathy for that young Johnny Big Balls, away from home for the first time getting a bit of freedom and literally going mad. Sure, God love him. Bizarrely, I did the show that night and performed pretty well. The Aussie praised my new-found focus. The crack must have been mighty.

Helen eventually couldn't deal with me anymore, so packed up her trunk and left the circus with about a week to go of the run, leaving me to dot the i's and cross the t's with the venue. (I couldn't blame her and, against all odds, we're still really good friends today.) Rather than take her departure as a sign that I needed to look at my behaviour, I was delighted. Because it meant even more freedom. The Dublin girls effectively became my producer and director. Rehearsals and production meetings were usually in pubs and nightclubs, and final-ising agreements with venues and the end of the run were done with the whole team off their game from the night before.

It was also the summer of love. The constant state of being out of my box gave me phenomenal Dutch courage with women. The Mauri woman running the hostel joked that I emerged from a different room every morning. But it wasn't sleazy. It was more like you'd fall in love with someone new every couple of days and fall asleep with them drinking cheap wine, talking guff and listening to tunes. There was a Catalan girl who wore a long white plastic coat. The Scottish and Irish girls used to mock her 'going out to milk the cows' in it. She was ludicrously beautiful and I got her clearly peeved male Catalan friend to translate a poem I wrote for her into her mother tongue. She didn't seem overly impressed by it. He probably mis-translated it out of envy, the prick. There was a 25-year-old Australian girl about whom me and Tipp had to have a serious conversation before I hooked up with her, as I'd never been with such a mature woman before. At the time, to me, twenty-five seemed like being on the precipice of qualifying for the bus pass. But my poor little heart was maybe taken most by a Cork girl. We'd drink and take Ecstasy together and just be really sweet and kind to each other. It was drug-fuelled but wholesome. It was back in the days when the pills were uncomplicated little buddies who just wanted to be your friend and make you feel nice.

Our only disagreement in Edinburgh was when she lost track of me for a while because I was inside the men's toilets kissing the mirror. Before the Narcissus fable pops into your head, I wasn't kissing myself thinking I was so great or handsome or anything, I was more showing myself a bit of pent-up love. That's my story and I'm sticking to it. As much as I absolutely adored drinking, it was hard to find time to kiss yourself in the mirror when you'd be out with the lads in the Quinn Ryan bar on Barrack Street. Ecstasy, before it turned on me, was really quite spiritual. Back on the dance floor with the Cork girl, we danced (well, she danced, I occasionally moved my hands and head) to the DJ-Sammy remix of Bryan Adams' 'Heaven' – sound of the summer. She asked me if I would go to her graduation ball and whispered in my ear still probably the nicest thing anyone's ever said to me: 'You have a beautiful mind.'

Edinburgh is also where my life-long love of Celtic Football Club really took off. To support myself (i.e. my drinking) during the run of the play, I worked on a construction site in Livingston. I arrived the first day with my long hair and Ireland World Cup 2002 jersey. One of the lads on the site said, 'Oh, look, it's Bobby fuckin' Sands.' Although I was aware of sectarian tensions in Scotland, I don't think anything can prepare you for how hostile and hateful it can be. Especially when you're a clueless, cocky, often drunk or spaced-out young Fenian. The guys I was initially put to work with inside were electricians and mostly Rangers supporters. They didn't really talk to me but would sometimes talk to each other looking at me and generally just tried to make me feel uncomfortable.

There was one guy, to be fair, who was really sound. He was from a British Protestant background but didn't get bogged down with what he described as 'the playground stuff'. I think we kind of bonded because he was sympathetic to me when I'd come in hardly fit to stand. He, though an excellent worker, used to drink cans throughout his lunch break to keep him going. I guess the foreman had nothing to say because he was such a good worker. This guy's hit the sweet spot, I remember thinking. He's constantly on the piss but he's still reliable, still excelling at what he does. I would spend the next fifteen years of my life trying, and failing, to emulate him.

After a few days in the electricians' Rangers' supporters club, I came in for my break and my Ireland jersey was on the ground covered in mud. I went to pick it up and it was sopping with piss. Someone in the hut saw what had happened and there was a bit of a kerfuffle. My cans-for-lunch buddy gave a few of the sparks a dressing-down. I wasn't mad about the pissy Ireland top but I was definitely enjoying being the centre of attention. Next thing I knew, I was moved outside digging and whatnot with a bunch of second-generation Irish, Celtic-mad lunatics. One of them was a famous Celtic fan called Badger, who told me he knew who the culprit was and that he had exacted revenge on my behalf in the individual's sandwich. I didn't ask. But I'll tell ya this: I was very happy to have the protection and love of my new crew.

Charlie from Falkirk took me under his wing. He had grandparents from Cork and we'd talk about West

Cork and Kerry and Donegal all day. He knew I was an absolutely useless worker so when I'd come in in a state, he'd make up a little bed for me with bubble wrap and insulation foil for the morning, and only get me back up for the break so I could annoy some of the Rangers fans with what was effectively a script he'd prepared for me: 'Jesus, Scotland's great, isn't it? I'm never going home to Ireland. Can't believe you get your dole on top of this. All my brothers are coming over now too . . . when they get out of jail.'

After lunch on a Saturday, if Celtic were at home, we'd drive to Glasgow, watch the match (Larsson and Sutton in their absolute pomp), and then he'd bring me home for haggis with his wife and drop me home to Edinburgh in the evening to do my show. He was so incredibly kind and paternal with me and we'd a great old bond. It's one of my regrets that many years later he came and knocked on my door in Cork and left a message for me. I think I just sent him some pissy excuse of a text instead of ringing him to meet up. I had just started one of my many attempts to stop drinking and I was terrified about going into pubs and just couldn't handle it. I thought he'd look down on me for not drinking anymore. If you're somehow reading this, Charlie in Falkirk – you were a big part of one of the best experiences of my life. Thank you for the craic and the kindness.

Chapter Seven

The Little Cub with Blinky Stretches

After that trip to Edinburgh, I worked in a factory in Ovens, County Cork, between my first and second years of college. I was twenty, still living at home but managing to block out the worst of the mother's mania by just focusing on myself and my new-found freedom. Without my dad to keep me in check, I lived like a renter and had my own personal fiefdom in my childhood bedroom. I had an old PlayStation, a copy of Pro Evolution Soccer and a few Aphex Twin and Autechre albums, and I was happy out with my circular life of bedroom, work and pub.

One night, before I got up for my shift, my girlfriend at the time called me on my mobile. I didn't answer because I was tired. But then she rang the home phone saying she wanted to meet up and talk about something. I asked her what could possibly be so urgent, 'You're not pregnant are you?' There was no reply.

I dismissively ended the call, saying something like we'd talk about it the following day. I went back to bed fairly sure my girlfriend was pregnant but I slept well. I went to work the next day and didn't think about the phone call much. Did it even happen? And even if it did, she could easily have done the tests wrong. Deny, dissociate. They had served me so well before.

At the break, I told my manager about the phone call. 'Has she taken a test?' he asked.

'Yeah, she's taken two, I think. Both positive. But they could be wrong, couldn't they?'

'Nah, man, I think they can only be wrong when they say they're NOT pregnant.'

Panic. Reality was darting through the blinds again, hurting my eyes. I met my girlfriend as soon as I finished work and we went to the doctor's for test three. Third time lucky, I thought. Myself and herself were mad about each other but we were kids and had been together merely months. The thought of bringing a child into the equation was ludicrous. That wouldn't suit my drinking or PlayStation-playing one jot.

As we waited for the results of the test, though, I thought about somebody else other than myself for the first time in nearly twenty-four hours. My nineteen-year-old girlfriend looked so scared and vulnerable waiting to hear what the doctor was going to say next. I put my arm around her and gratefully accepted the doctor's approving smile. The doctor confirmed the pregnancy and gave us some leaflets and perfunctory advice about our next steps but I zoned out, like someone in a film receiving bad news. Was there anything to be said for a fourth test?

I can only imagine how difficult it must have been for my young girlfriend, unexpectedly pregnant with her first child and dealing with an absolute balm-pot like me. Monday I'd be assuring her and her little bump that I'd be the best dad since God the Father, and I'd mean it, every word. By Tuesday I'd be up a tree somewhere after taking ketamine. Addiction is complex. I believe in order to be useful you need empathy for the person struggling with it; you must try to get an understanding of the pain they carry, a pain so great they need to be off their head most of the time. In fact, that's a big part of the reason I wrote this book. But addiction, for me at least, was/is incredibly selfish too. After I picked up the first drink, I'd hand over control. There was genuinely not a whole lot I could do when the physical craving for more kicked in. But before going back on the piss, I always had some control, I always had choices. I was often only too aware of the pain it would cause other people but time and again, I chose to do it anyway. On balance, I'd choose the good feelings drink was going to give me and accept the bad feelings it would give others as collateral. For me – and this is just my experience – it was vital for my recovery to acknowledge that selfishness, to take responsibility for it and to not allow myself to become a victim of nature or nurture (or lack thereof).

And so, while the early months of pregnancy were as chaotic as ever, something did change in the run in to Caoimhe's arrival. I was able to rein myself in due to the enormity of the situation we found ourselves in and a bit of basic human compassion for my partner. I stopped drinking. I quit college and went full-time in that factory to try to gather together some cash, as the word on the street was that kids were costly. I started becoming interested, enthusiastic about fatherhood.

Just as well, because one beautiful spring morning in 2004, in St Finbarr's Hospital, my daughter stormed into the world, kicking and screaming. The midwife placed her in the glass cot and told me I could say hello. I tentatively approached her and put my little finger into her hand and she clutched it like it was a lifebuoy. We had connected. From the get-go I was just stunned by her. I couldn't stop looking at her perfect, tiny head. That I had anything at all to do with bringing this little cherub into being was astonishing to me. I had definitely done something worthwhile now – here was proof. Tears streamed down my face. It was like nothing before this moment counted. A clean slate, a fresh start invented by love. This beautiful little creature was in this world now and I was her dad. I wasn't the co-conspirator in the creation of a bump anymore. I was a father to this tiny cub holding onto my finger for dear life, contorting, yawning with blinky stretches. I'd never felt love like it before. I had a purpose now: I was going to be the greatest dad in the history of Cork.

And for a time, I would have given dads everywhere a run for their money. Despite my brothers taking the piss out of me, I was changing nappies (unprecedented behaviour where I grew up) and pushing buggies. I just loved spending time with her and felt really proud to be associated with her. She was so beautiful that there would have to be something wrong with you if you weren't in love with her. Her mother had great taste and used to dress her in these mini vintage coats and jackets and I can forever picture her in this chic purple coat with big buttons, up in my arms with her chubby cheeks and her brilliant blue eyes. But she wasn't just a cute doll, she was also a high-octane action hero. I remember her storming around my mother's house at about two or three years of age in her knickers after tearing off her dress, pretending she was a monkey. Saucy face up on her, swinging from couch to couch. She cracked my mother up. In fact, most of the bright moments that I can recall from the last decade of my mother's life involve Caoimhe.

I have a home video from the day of Caoimhe's communion. We rented a bouncy castle and put it up in Mam's back garden. Mam really made an effort on the day (or my sister made it for her) and she looks beautiful. There's a lovely bit with her and Caoimhe messing together in the house. My mother didn't laugh too often but when she did, she'd shake with it, genuinely from the belly. I'm blessed to have that clip. It's like a snapshot of how things could or should have always been: me being a consistent father, my mother being present and not fearful and bothered.

My mam was just different with Caoimhe. I genuinely don't remember her ever being drunk around her; in fact, years later, she and my sister plugged many a gap in my parenting caused by my own addiction. Her face would light up when Caoimhe bounded into the house.

Caoimhe would make up fantastical stories in which she would play all the parts. Like father, like daughter. My mother would egg her on and laugh hysterically at the witchy faces she'd make when she was playing baddies. Mam would become childlike once again, as she had been before she became terrified by life, or more pertinently, her own mind.

And for my own part, myself and the cherub instantly became best buddies. When I'd come home from work in the factory she'd scramble across the floor of the apartment with a big, beautiful, excited head up on her, frantically trying to climb up my leg and into my arms. My heart is light even thinking about it now. When she got a little older we'd bounce around Cork city together, hopping on school buses or my bicycle with her ladyship on the crossbar, getting up to shenanigans, having the craic. I was probably more like a friend than a father to her but I was obsessed with her nonetheless, and I reckon she single-handedly kept me sane and soberish for a long time. Maybe even alive.

I remember bringing her to Salthill in Galway on the bus when she was about six. I think it was my first time taking her outside Cork on my own and I really wanted it to be special for her. I told her that for the next few days we'd do whatever she wanted to do. She instantly became drunk with power. It was midsummer and we played on the beach and paddled till about half past nine at night. We got back to the B&B and I washed the sand off her legs. She got into her nightie and brushed her teeth and unexpectedly started settling down for the evening. The lights went off and everything. 'Goodnight, Dad.'

'Goodnight,' said I, partially in shock. This all seemed a bit too good to be true. I threw on the reading lamp, lay back on my bed and got my book out. Before I'd even read a page, I heard a sigh coming from the bed beside me.

Me: What's wrong?
C: I can't sleep.
Me: You're trying less than a minute.
Silence.
C: Do you think we came away from the beach too soon?
Me: I don't think so. We were there nearly two-and-a-half hours.
C: I think we did.
Silence.
C: I think we should go back.
Me: What? Sure, you're washed and in your nightie now and in bed. That's crazy!
C: I thought we were gonna do whatever I wanted to do?

Checkmate. Back to the beach in semi-darkness.

When I'd looked into her cot that spring morning, I thought to myself, *This is it now, I'm cured. There's no way I'm going to go missing for days again. I love her a thousand times more than the best party I've ever been to. I'm on the straight and narrow.* But it didn't last. In

116

time, I started to feel edgy. I got bored. The gloss seemed to wear off pushing buggies and changing nappies. And so I started drinking again. Not chaotically at first. I was desperate to manage it this time. I was desperate to be a good father, one who just happened to have a few drinks at the weekend. But I kind of knew in the depths of me that I couldn't have my drink and drink it.

After Edinburgh and into fatherhood, very little changed. Much of my twenties, even going into my early thirties, was chaotic and self-destructive – but, again, often great craic. My partner and I had split up and I'd moved out. I tried to set up a life for myself where I could see my daughter when I was clear-headed and it suited me, but where I'd also have leeway to get wrecked when the time came. And the time came regularly. It's not a particularly pleasant thing to admit but in a period in which going missing for several days to go on binges became a semi-regular occurrence, with all the worry and hassle that it caused my family, I was still enjoying myself. It's not like I didn't care, of course I did – I was just too wrapped up in myself and the sweet release of being blind drunk to bother.

By now, I was in a band who had some critical success. Exit: Pursued by a Bear, we were called, God love us. *Winter's Tale* reference. Read a book, will you? 'You'll never sell records with a name like that,' they said. And they were so, so right. But that suited me down to the ground. Selling records was for capitalist scumbags. The critically successful were misunderstood by the masses and came into their own at small gatherings around the gaffs, nightclubs and early houses of Cork.

The band were touring Ireland at one point and barely speaking to me as I traipsed after them with my partner at the time and D (still my partner in crime) on a seemingly never-ending bender. My bandmates would arrive and set up the gear; I'd come in barely able to speak let alone sing after being up all night drinking and roaring. We'd do a unsatisfactory gig where I'd croak and wipe the sweat off my forehead for a bit. Then the bemused audience would file out, the band would pack up the gear and hop into the van, and I'd travel separately onto the next town to continue the festivities.

One night, me and D were at a party somewhere in Cork, I think, and we were going through a period where if we were in the company of a so-inclined girl or lad, we'd get our make-up done. My God, we loved getting our make-up done. We 'love to look pretty', as D clarified. On this occasion we'd been up all night drinking and the band had a gig in Galway the following day. So along with our other good buddy F, D and I drove to Galway with no tax, no insurance, one of the windows permanently jammed down, our faces covered in make-up and drunk from the night before. Our pockets were full of drugs and the bang of weed out of the car was no one's business. But it was about to become the Garda Síochána's business.

About halfway up to Galway, a squad car pulled us over. Mine and F's usual playful bravado escaped us: he clutched my hand and whispered in my ear very, very slowly, as if this would somehow need to be delicately explained to me: 'We're fucked.'

'Yeah, I know.'

Guard, peering in the driver's window: What are ye up to, lads?

D: We're off to Galway to play a gig.

Guard: Where in Galway?

D: Cellar Bar.

Guard: Kinda music is it?

D: Kinda glam rock kind of stuff.

Guard, seeming to be getting into it: Hence the make-up . . .

D: That's right.

Guard: Well, lads, ye've no tax, ye've no insurance and yer window is bust.

D: I tell ya, Guard, the band's van broke down and we had to travel separately so I had to take this out on the road. We were in a rush to get to the event because it's an all-ages gig and we don't want to let the kids down. I'll get everything sorted tomorrow.

Guard: The two lads in the back are very quiet, aren't they?

(I thought to myself: *You'd be quiet too if you had a farting, panicking man next to you clutching your hand and silently saying 'Oh God' every now and then.*)

D: Don't worry about them, they're the shy types. I'm the front man, you see.

(I suddenly realised that D was playing out a fantasy here.)

Guard: Alright lads, get it sorted tomorrow now, d'ya hear?

D: Thanks a million, Guard.

BEAT

Guard: What's that smell?

(*Oh no. Oh Christ. We were so close.*)

D: I dunno, Guard. C'mere, we better be . . .

(The guard continued smelling.)

Guard: Fuckin' hell, that'd knock ya out.

D: It wasn't me, anyway, Guard, I don't smoke at all.

(*Fucking hell, D's hanging us out to dry here*, I thought.)

Guard: Smoke? I wish. No, there's an awful smell of shit.

D: Ah, one of the lads is from West Cork, check your boots you will ya, F?

(The guard chuckled. D had played the role of his life.)

D. Anyway, Guard, I might see ya up there, will I?

And bang, we were on the road again.

Chapter Eight

When the Gat Goes Flat

*But, at the end of the day, I'm an alcoholic, my
friends, and Christmas is the one time of the year
that our drinking seems somewhat normal. And so
Fearg is barely up the stairs – and it's can o'clock,
the blinds are pulled, Titanic is on, and I'm roaring
crying. Fifteen, twenty cans later, the sun is peek-
ing back in, I'm three sheets to the wind and who's
coming down the stairs in an Adidas tracksuit and
runners, all set for the fun run – only my turkey
buddy Feargal. I play the game. I put my runners
on – empty cans, ashtrays; falling all over the place,
onto the beautiful Christmas tree, blocking out the
lovely light we created together. And I look over and
Feargal's stood there and his waddle is purple. I say,
'Fearg, purple? You're beyond angry are ya, buddy?
You're enraged are ya?' He goes, 'I'm not, pal, purple means ... disappointed.' Wow. I was used to
letting myself down but now I was after letting my
best buddy down too.*

From *In One Eye, Out the Other*

I wasn't a regular whiskey drinker. Though I loved its promise of wild abandon, the unpredictability, the aggression – the sheer twistedness it visited on my mind – constituted a lot of baggage even for me. Parking personal accountability for just a moment; it was a dance with the devil and by far the most dangerous drug I ever used. I don't remember ever pissing myself, blacking out or getting barred from pubs after random acts of violence on Ecstasy or mushrooms.

Though you'd be away with the fairies, there were times when my whiskey-fuelled antics were more ridiculous than anything. I remember getting barred from three pubs in Cork in the space of one afternoon. In each one, I'd storm in, throw my sister's leather jacket on the ground, and challenge the entire bar to fistycuffs. For clarity, we're talking daytime drinking of a Tuesday here, so there might just be one auld lad nursing a Guinness in the corner. Thank God for the ejections though because if it kicked off, my money would be on him – I fight like a toddler warding off tickles.

Another night I was jettisoned out of a nightclub for calling an incandescent bouncer a 'virgin'. I taunted him that only an actual virgin would be getting this worked up about it. We exchanged pushes and next thing I was on the ground with my head pressed against the pavement. Shortly afterwards I found myself in a *garda* (police) car. Back at the police station, I charmed the pants off the guards, or so I believed. There were three dank unoccupied cells available and one of the guards said I could take my pick. I said, 'Ooh that's a tough one, they all look so appealing.' We both laughed. By this time, D with characteristic solidarity, had started giving the virgin bouncer lip and soon found himself in the cell next door to mine. D and I had a top laugh with the guards and they let us out at dawn in time for opening hours in Charlie's bar. I thought no more of it until a *garda* car called to my mother's house a week or so later and frightened the shit out of her. They'd come to deliver me a summons for drunken disorderly. Be careful, kids: next time you find yourself having what you believe is a great time with law enforcement – you may just have been drinking whiskey all day.

I was on the Powers one day with my brother Alan in a pub on Bandon Road. This was when my ex was heavily pregnant with Caoimhe, and she came in to say hello. When an old lad in the pub didn't get up to let her sit down as quickly as I would have liked, I laid into him verbally, effing and blinding at him.

'What's wrong with you? That's no way to talk to an old man,' said my brother. 'Go over and—'

'Who are you to tell me how to behave, you stupid prick?' I shot back. 'Get out of my face.'

I adore my brother, he is razor sharp and, unlike me, has had a good job all his life. Though I was younger and possibly fitter, the man could have beaten me like a bowl of eggs had he so wished, but it wasn't that that made me fearful and tortured the next day when I came round. It was the thought of not being fully sure what I was capable of when out of my mind. I remember trying to explain to him the next day that my words had meant nothing but I could see an understandable glimmer of doubt in his eyes. I suppose he didn't generally behave erratically and maliciously when drunk, so he found it hard to understand why his little brother, whom he loved and who loved him, would do so.

When I was away from home for the first time in Edinburgh he wrote to me once to tell me about how things were going in Cork, wondering how I was getting on. I was flummoxed. He wasn't a letter-sender. We weren't a letter-sending family. That he had gone to the effort of composing and sending that letter brought me to tears in that youth hostel in Leith. That I could besmirch this bond by acting out in the way I did was tough to take. I was behaving completely contrary to my values and beliefs and this disturbed me to my core. But not enough to stop drinking.

The love I had for drinking cannot be confined to funny or wild stories from any particular place or time. It was the overall feeling of sureness it gave me. A feeling of safety and security that the fears and feelings were back in their box – I'd had my spinach and I was on my way. From eighteen onwards I was always 'breaking out'. I'd be off alcohol for a period and then would go back on it unexpectedly. My dry time had passed and I would afford myself the opportunity, the reward of a well-deserved celebration.

The first night back on the sauce was usually tense and anticlimactic. I would've been building up to it so much in my head that it could never possibly fulfil expectations.

Also, try as I might to block it out, I couldn't shake the awareness that what I was doing was bad for me and for the people who cared for me, and so, as the years went on, from my twenties into my thirties, it was very hard to enjoy myself until I got good and wrecked and passed out. When I woke the next morning I'd have an overwhelming craving for more alcohol. It's probably an odd thing to say but I partly loved that craving. And if I could have somehow siphoned the feeling to the people in my life who quite reasonably thought I was just a selfish prick, they might have been able to understand my lack of power after I picked up a drink again. It was futile even attempting to put up any kind of battle, and there was a certain peace in that.

So, the morning after the night before was always my favourite time. It started by me rallying the troops on floors and couches, sending texts, getting a nice gang together to hit the early-morning house by 7.30 at the latest and have a good run at it. As odd as this might sound to you, I actually have butterflies in my stomach right now even recalling how excited I'd be, assembling my team, gearing up to have another day in paradise with my forever friend, blacking out the world, the feelings, the responsibilities, the shame and the self-loathing. What's not to like? In the theatre of the early-morning house, I was a lead character: devilishly handsome, impossibly hilarious, a lothario, a poet who never wrote.

I loved opening the door and it whooshing closed behind me, protecting me from the world. I had gained entry to the secret society, the place where all the normal people battling weather, traffic and unsatisfactory relationships would surely love to be if they only had the balls. I loved the banter, the edgy, wanton buffoonery that seemed to have equal measures love and hate pouring into it. I loved sneaking into the toilet and taking whatever drug was around on the day – never because of any real affinity for the powder, just so I could stay awake to drink. I loved the taste, particularly of Beamish stout; I was both director and audience to its disappearing act in the glass, and I loved the browny, dirty cream clinging onto the sides for dear life. And the smell, particularly of whiskey and its promise, its guarantee to take you out, transport you somewhere else and give you blind valour. A lot of the time I even loved hangovers, as long as they didn't have the ol' pesky suicidal depression or anxiety lurking behind them. More often than not, I'd just wake up with what I can best describe as a wacky head. It would be almost enjoyable because even though I might have felt physically sick or my head might have been pounding, I knew that very soon I'd be going for a drink and that would take it all away.

I remember someone in recovery circles saying that one time and it really struck a chord. He'd been drinking the night before, he said, and woke up feeling really shaky, wondering whether or not he'd be able to go to work that morning. He managed to get to the house he was working in and, much to his relief, there happened to be four cans on the kitchen table. He didn't need to drink them to be assuaged. The sight of them was enough to reassure him. In my case, just being around alcohol, having the potential for getting drunk again, the promise of it, would often be enough to sustain me and keep me detached from reality or myself. Because it's more accurate to say that I longed to remove myself from my reality – it was this and not the outside world from which I was constantly running away from. Sitting in Charlie's bar next to the fire, Wikiquoting Hobbes and Joyce, or Wolfe Tone, with a belly full of drink and a pocket full of drugs, I felt released from the pressures pushing down on me, within me. It was a sweet release and I did everything but die in the pursuit of that feeling.

For all the trouble and pain and drama it was causing me, I simply couldn't imagine a world in which I wasn't using alcohol to manage my moods. I was Gatman after all, and drink gave me my superpowers. With a few drinks in me, I could be in the thick of trouble, not a bother on me, threatening and promising big, delivering little. I was the type of drunk who'd start fights but would then be slipping out the back door when it was kicking off. I'd be onto the next pub. One of my most enjoyable morning's drinking had to be when I befriended an Afro-English kickboxer who was over in Cork on holidays. We just went around the pubs of the city, me starting fights, him finishing them.

I also honestly don't know if I ever would've had the confidence to even speak to a woman were it not for booze. Because I was so fearful and insecure, and was negotiating the world with this flamboyant but flimsy ego, my strategy with the cailíní was very clear: get drunk. That was it. Usually, when drunk, I'd find myself in scenarios in which chatting to girls I liked just seemed to happen without me having to do anything. It was like little mini voluntary blackouts. Get enough down the hatch – not too much, mind you, don't wanna overdo it – and you never really have to consciously put yourself out there and run the risk of rejection.

My wish list for a romantic partner was short and sweet: do they like me? End of list. As in, really like me enough to put up with my drinking and behaviour, and, more importantly, enough to reassure me that I won't be rejected by them? If so, play ball; if not, thanks for your time but sorry, I'm up the walls at the moment.

When I told a friend I was writing this book, he asked me, 'What's the difference between you and me, though? Why are you an alcoholic when I used to drink as much as you and stay awake for days taking drugs and everything?' I think the difference between the two of us is closely connected to how we felt just before we stopped. My buddy said he stopped because he really just got sick of it; he became bored and tired and cranky pulling all-nighters and believed he'd be a better worker and partner if he were to knock the partying on the head. He said that when he decided he'd had enough, he literally just stopped overnight. My buddy's decision-making was logical. He weighed up the pros and cons and made a rational decision according to the data. Having reached solid conclusions, he put his findings into action with immediate effect with little or no trouble.

That was not my experience. When I eventually stopped drinking there was no exploring evidence or rational decision-making. Well, perhaps there was one decision: I decided I wanted to live. I became 100 per cent convinced that if I continued to drink, I would die. It might be on the next bender or sometime in the future, but I had passed the point of no return in my journey with drinking to cope. I had all these feelings and fears and they hadn't gone away, but I had slowly come to the terrifying conclusion that drink was no longer helping me to bury them. There was a metaphorical gun to my head: keep drinking and die or stop and have a chance at some kind of life.

Unlike my friend, I needed the support of an army of other alcoholics, friends and family, therapy, and a source of strength from something greater than myself to have any chance of actually stopping. And so maybe that's the difference between the party person and the addict: want versus need. My friend wanted to party; then he wanted to be a good partner and improve his career, so he stopped. I needed to drink and do drugs because I found it untenable being me, living in my head. I stopped not because I wanted to but because I needed to stay alive, if not for myself initially, then certainly for Caoimhe.

Throughout my twenties there were many times when my drinking and drug-taking got in the way of basic parental responsibilities. My ex-partner understandably wanted to protect my daughter from the continued disappointments of me not showing up for her, and so there were brief but painful periods where I wouldn't see her, in the hope that I would go away, get my shit together and come back ready to finally be the consistent, reliable father my daughter needed.

In 2007 I got my first gig with RTÉ. It was a live kids' TV show called *Sattitude*. I started as a chaperone helping out with the kids and cleaning up afterwards, but in no time I wormed my way in front of the camera, making cameos as a studio-assistant dolt named Tim, who'd forget things, stumble and stutter over his words. Tim was well received and I was asked to officially join the cast. I received a script for the following week and was beside myself to learn that Tim would end up being destroyed in gunge at the end of the episode. I immediately thought of my daughter. She was gonna love it. After another painful hiatus she was back in my life as I'd been dry for a few months. Myself and herself spent hours discussing the gunge and speculating on the process of getting it off myself and the studio afterwards. She was giddy about the big day.

The night before my appearance on the show, I was buzzing. Friends and family sent me texts to say that they'd be watching in the morning. Next thing I was sitting at home and I got a text from the lads. They were in a pool hall having one or two. I knew I shouldn't be anywhere near a pub the night before a show – I wasn't an idiot – but two mitigating circumstances came to mind: one, they were playing pool. It wouldn't just be a load of lads in a dark corner drinking pints and talking guff. As a shit-hot pool player, I could slip in, give the lads a bit of a spanking, head off again, sober, like some sort of reformed, 'don't even miss it anymore', success story. And two, even though I'd landed a bit part on a low-budget Saturday morning kids' TV show, where the sole purpose of my character was to have pink or green shite dumped on me every week, in my head I was Cillian Murphy. It'd be nice for the lads to rub shoulders with me, get a sense of my process, my rider, etc.

So, even though I'd been off it for months, had my family back in my life and was on the eve of the biggest work opportunity I could have dreamed of, I somehow decided that it was worth going back into the burning building I'd somehow managed to escape from.

At first there was no issue. I was on the orange juice, talking TV, hammering the lads on the table and feeling fairly comfortable. J wasn't drinking either, so D was on the lash for the three of us. Next thing, who walked in the door and set up at the table next to us with his buddy? Only Roy Keane. Me and the lads were trying to keep it together but our heads were gone. Keane's buddy set up for the first game and the man himself slipped into the toilet. His walk to the jacks was a venerable spectacle in itself: back arched, head up, like a gladiator walking into battle. It reminded me so much of my old man. Was this a sign? Alkies are always looking for signs. Does this mean I should drink? Or shouldn't? I was on the lookout for anything that would take the responsibility away from me.

Meanwhile, me, J and an already-flaming-drunk D held a whispered council about Keano. The feeling was that we couldn't let this opportunity go and it was decreed that it should be me to follow the gladiator into the men's, to tell him how much we all loved him. I can't remember why this was decided or what we imagined would be the ideal outcome but, anyway, I found myself following a notoriously volatile man into a tiny pool-hall toilet.

So, I stood there trembling behind the arched back. Keane was orchestrating a pee with the same level of precision and dedication with which he'd run the Manchester United midfield for a decade. As absolutely shitting myself though I was, I employed a fairly robust logic: knowing well that when he finished this pee, odds on he was going to make his way towards me, I loitered by the sink. The pee was long. Various thoughts ran through my panicked, mental little head: *Oh, he must have been bursting to go, that's why he ran in before even taking a shot.* And, *This is a weird place to start a friendship. I bet in years to come, Roy Keane will be telling people, 'I first became best friends with Tadhg Hickey when he followed me into the toilet one night!'*

Suddenly, the pee stopped and the surely magic moment was at hand. He turned and looked at me. I looked at him. I opened my mouth to begin to tell him what exactly I'll never know. But before I could get the first syllable past my chattering teeth, he gave me this look. Not a particularly aggressive one, not even a peevish glance, but one that seemed to say, *Don't do this. Please leave. The end.* I gave him a nod and bolted.

I didn't even have it in me to make up some bullshit alternative version of events to the buddies. I just told them the truth. They laughed, I laughed and we headed to the pub next door for more discreet post-match analysis. There I felt something I hadn't felt in months: the wild abandon of the craic in the pub. Sobriety had offered me nothing like that yet; it just felt like work, tedious, never-ending work, and the payment was just pats on the back. My true self, or so I told myself now, was to be in the thick of the craic with the lads and the girls, having a few pints, having high-jinks toilet escapades with childhood heroes. And what harm would one or two be now? I mean, I wasn't going to stay out when there was something this important on the next day. That would be insanity.

J had now gone and I reasoned that a drunken D wouldn't even notice if I ordered a real drink or not. I approached the counter and time stood still. To my left, an entire musical theatre number had started up with most of the bar involved. The tune was called 'What's the Harm?' and by the end, all the staff were up on the counter giving it socks: 'You're entitled to the one, what is life if it's not fun – so what's the HARRRRM??!' I looked to my right and this floor-emptying, morose, country-music dirge was trying to compete, bleating something about 'staying on the water wagon, taking the straight road'.

The next thing I remember was coming to in a house somewhere, clutching a bottle of brandy, with D and people I didn't know, watching the television programme I should have been on. They were laughing their heads off. I tapped my pockets: no phone, no keys, no excuses. Good boy done bad. Very bad. The penance for this one was going to be the worst yet. And with that in mind, I figured that there was no point throwing in the towel for a while. I was watching a TV show in which I was a character who hadn't turned up. I might as well be hung for a sheep as a lamb, I thought. And so I put the bottle of brandy to my lips and closed my eyes.

By my late twenties the drinking and the 'partying' had almost become humdrum. What seemed anarchic and exhilarating in my early twenties now seemed like a formula for numbness and self-delusion. When I was with the lads, we'd repeat the same jokes and stories on a loop: 'best of the sesh', if you will. We were playing the hits over and over till you started to hate the sound of them. It seemed to me that the lads were drinking to remember but I'd already started drinking to forget. When the session ended the depression and anxiety were no one's business, literally. I never talked to anyone about it because it felt to me like a fairly straightforward punishment for my lifestyle choices. I had enjoyed the dirty picture so now it was time for the mouthful of snakes. And so it reinforced the idea of the double life: the good boy who sent his next-door neighbour a condolence card when her dog passed away and the bad boy who chose drink over his daughter, time and time again.

Occasionally, the good boy/bad boy worlds collided. I remember turning my phone off during a bender. I had promised to take my daughter for the night but I didn't want the possibility of frustrated calls or texts from my ex wrecking my beer buzz. That night, when I stumbled home to whatever shitty gaff I was staying in at the time and was just about to fall asleep, I turned the phone on to find missed calls and texts from staff at the Cope Foundation. My brother Con had been rushed to hospital. This would happen sporadically. He had had another epileptic fit but was not recovering as he normally would. An ambulance had been called and a family member needed to be with him. Con had been written off time and time again over the years by doctors but had always powered through. Now in his late thirties, he had smashed his life expectancy, but on these occasions, you naturally feared the worst. I had a great relationship with the Cope staff, making sure to hide my failings as a father and addiction issues from them. To them, there was no good boy/bad boy dichotomy. I was just a good boy, and the good boy had made himself their primary point of contact.

What to do? I was drunk out of my mind, and not energetic, fun-times drunk, more like been-out-for-two-days-desperately-needing-sleep drunk. But my brother could be dying in hospital and it was too late to try to get someone else to go in my stead. I decided I needed to get out there. I remember pulling my pushbike out of the shed (because I hadn't been bothered to learn to drive) and cycling the few miles out to Cork University Hospital, falling off more than once, tying the bike up and slapping myself rigorously across the face, as if I could somehow slap the two days of drinking out of me.

I needn't have worried because if there's one word I'd use to describe sitting up till dawn in an Irish A&E on a Saturday night it'd be 'sobering'. As I slumped on a plastic chair, holding my largely unresponsive brother's hand, listening to the drunken nonsense and sometimes abuse the nurses were enduring outside the curtain, I experienced the brutal phenomenon of being compelled to stay awake while unmedicated. My unmerciful hangover and delirium tremens kicked in and I promised myself and the world I would never drink again.

A staff member from Cope arrived in the morning to tag me out. On this occasion Con pulled through and shrugged off the whole experience. So did I. I was back in the pub that evening.

Con finally passed away in 2010. The family were summoned to his bedside in Cope on the Sunday as he was receiving the last rites, but with typical Hickey swagger and defiance, he hung on until the following Thursday – the occasion of his fortieth birthday. He was a sucker for the attention like myself, I reckon. In those few days, crammed into his room in Cope, the Hickeys laughed, cried, consoled and I think understood each other in a way we hadn't done before or maybe since. He brought us all together and then he left us. I still miss him.

Chapter Nine

The Jumping-off Place

Fearg sits down next to me and takes me under his wing. 'Look, man, would you ever just drop the act?' he says. 'There's no way you could be happy-go-lucky after going through what you went through – would you ever just stop drinking for one second and just talk about it? I'm here for you buddy – I'm listening.' He's pouring cans down the sink. 'If you sort yourself out now, Feargal, you really will be 'Fear Gal' because your future's going to be so bright. I promise you: the best is yet to come.'

From *In One Eye, Out the Other*

By my late twenties I was in this hamster wheel, either off it and trying to make it up to everyone, or on it and causing carnage. One weekend I was supposed to have my now-eight-year-old daughter again because her mother was away with work. I'd been really looking forward to it; we were going to make a cake, which I was super pumped about because I'd never done any baking before. She was going to lead the operation and my main responsibility would be to keep her from standing too close to the oven. I'd been in good-boy mode for a while, so there was no real fear either from me or my family that I wouldn't be up to it. Again, I think I'd made that mistake of believing that my love for my daughter would supersede my perpetual longing to be off my head.

It was arranged that her mum would drop Caoimhe to me at my mother's house early on Saturday morning. I went out on the Friday night to meet a friend who was over for the weekend from London. I wasn't drinking and actually felt quite smug in myself. Here I was, the only one of the lads not drinking, getting up in the morning to look after his kid while they'd all be nursing hangovers. What a dad. 'You're very sensible these days, Hickey,' they'd say, to which I'd reply, 'Responsibilities, lads. I'm a new man, sure.'

I trotted home early and on my way, came across a party hopping on College Road. Just as I was looking at it and again feeling quite smug that it wasn't me getting trapped in the rabbit hole this evening, one of the two young fellas chatting in the garden spotted me. 'Tadhg!' It was a lad from work. At the time, I was working part-time for a waste-management service, knocking door to door. The work was soul destroying but, bizarrely, I was good at it. Some of the young people working with me were lovely. Here was one of them, who kind of looked up to me; largely, I think, because he'd heard stories about me being 'mad'. He invited me in and I thought, *What's the harm? I'm not drinking; I'll come in, get a quick sense of what the youngsters are up to these days and leave them with some parting wisdom. It is still, after all, early.*

His place, one of those Victorian houses that had seen better days, was a quintessential party house or 'sesh gaff': a spacious living room for dancing and an assortment of other psychonaut shenanigans, and a shite, poky kitchen that looked like it hadn't seen many improvements in the century since the bauld Victoria had shuffled off, currently only being utilised for cutting up lines of coke and ketamine. People were asleep on the stairs or hanging off bannisters showing off to each other. Some lad was making an absolute fool out of himself trying to impress some clearly uninterested girl who was wandering in and out of the kitchen, much keener on sorting herself out with another line than listening to him. I understood this world very well and I could hold my own in it with the best of them.

I was standing in the hallway about to leave when my friend and his girlfriend dropped some comment along the lines of, 'I thought you were supposed to be a mad yoke!' That stung. It sounded like a bit of a dare and Mama didn't raise no quitter: she raised a horribly traumatised alcoholic. Next thing I remember, I was in the Savoy Nightclub and the DJ, Dave Clarke, was in the main space, a massive coup for Cork to coincide with a massive mistake for Tadhg. And though I was off my head on blue ghost yokes (Ecstasy) and cider, I was in that delusional space where I was assuring myself I'd be down off everything in a few hours and be home for a shower and a nap before my daughter was dropped off. And I really believed it too; I was convinced of it. I obsessively wanted to be able to do both things well: party and parent. And because I was an egomaniac and a fantasist, right up until the bitter end, I genuinely believed that any moment now I would figure out a way of doing it all. I just hadn't been thinking hard enough.

I was on the dance floor and I'd lost all the youngsters already. And I saw this girl glancing over towards me. With no drink or drugs in my system, I'd probably have looked behind me to see who she was looking at, and promptly and politely get out of her way. But when I was full of spinach like this, even though she was dancing with what looked like her boyfriend, a large, muscular European type, I slowly walked towards her and took her hand. The European gym bunny was so flummoxed he didn't do anything and the girl and I just slowly strolled out of the club together.

Walking through the city chatting and wondering what had just happened, we found ourselves up the northside where there was a party house I knew that was sure to be in full swing with people who were too mangled to make it to the club. The girl was from Guadeloupe and though she had broken English, she was evidently kind and adorable and beautiful.

The first few hours in the gaff were brilliant. I was the perfect gentleman, protecting her from lads and lassies who were falling about the place on various pills and powders. She'd only been in Cork a week and although she was accustomed to party scenes generally, there really is something unique about the Cork City variety. As demented and debauched as Galway but without the hippies and stench of health-food stores taking the edge off.

As the hours rolled by, my own edge was getting sharper because I knew what was coming. The girl wondered if we might see each other tomorrow and just wanted to go home to her hostel now, a ten-minute walk from where we were. Because she didn't really know Cork, she asked me to walk her back. I refused. She was reduced to pleading with me tearfully. I felt that with the drink and the amount of drugs I'd taken, I was kind of mentally stable and if I got up to walk her home and the cool air hit me, reality could kick in a bit too soon and I'd descend into panic. It just suited me better to stay put. I can still see the sad, confused and scared look on her face as she left the party to try to find her way back, alone. The next thing I remember is the first flushes of daylight coming through the window and my ex-girlfriend ringing me on repeat. There was half a bottle of someone else's beer on the table next to me, so I turned off my phone yet again and chugged it down as quickly as I could get it into my system.

I only remember bits and pieces of the rest of the weekend. I ended up back at the Victorian house sitting in a bedroom with no shoes on coming out of a blackout, asking whoever I was with what day it was. It was the early hours of Monday morning. *Jesus Christ.* I've heard this analogy used before and it's so accurate. Having a drink and drug problem is a bit like having a twin brother who hates you. He just does whatever the fuck he wants, creates utter carnage and despair everywhere he goes, just for kicks. And then when the fallout happens, he's left the scene and you're alone to pick up the pieces and mend the bridges. And you resent him so much because it seems like you never get any of the fun parts; you've no life of your own, actually. You're just anxiously waiting for him to kick off again and, as the years go on, you start to become terrified that the next time he breaks out could be the end of both of you.

I searched the house in a panic but my shoes were nowhere to be seen. And so I left without them. I walked the dawn streets and tried to sneak into my mother's house without her hearing me. In that moment, I truly loathed myself; I didn't feel that I was worthy of any compassion or understanding. I was just a lowlife – the drink problem was an excuse. I was a waste of space and I only kept chugging on out of cowardly terror of opting out. Because I would have loved to. I'd have absolutely rather been dead rather than show my face to these mad-with-worry people who loved me again. *What on earth am I going to say to my beautiful little daughter?* The excuse that I was just a bit young and wild was out the window – I was nearly thirty at this point; I'd started hanging out with people younger than me and if crawling through the toilet window with no shoes on was kind of funny coming from a fella in first year arts, it was more tragic when you were a grown man with a child who depended on you to be reliable, mentally stable and capable of love.

That day I made the usual apologies and put the pieces together of the time I'd been away to find out that my brother Dec and his wife had been looking after Caoimhe in my absence. The good boy done bad bought some flowers for my sister-in-law and headed up to their house to deliver them. At this stage, I really wasn't believing my own bullshit anymore so it would have been churlish to expect other people to believe it. The flowers were received meekly but when I walked in the door, I didn't recognise a couple of people in the front room and I quickly realised that I'd inadvertently stumbled into an intervention (of sorts) in my honour. Dec had had similar issues with alcohol in his younger years but had been sober now for years. He'd a couple of mates with him who were recovering from alcoholism and were willing to talk to me if I so wanted. It's probably worth noting that my mother played no part in this event. She undoubtedly wanted me to stop going missing for days on end due to the effect it was having on her nerves but I don't ever remember her suggesting I seek help for my drinking problem. I grew up in that infamous 1980s/90s Catholic Ireland spirit of secrecy. My mother's attitude was that seeking help and admitting you had a problem outside the sanctity of the house was shameful. Drinking your head off was OK as long as you weren't worrying your mam into an early grave.

One time when I was living with her, I woke up in a hedge at the end of our street with no shoes or trousers on (again with the shoes-losing). I'd been on a bender for the week and when I eventually ducked and dived through the neighbourhood, covering my underpants with bits of hedge like a pisshead Adam or Eve, and into the mother's, I said: 'Mam, I think I need to go to AA or something.' To which she replied, 'What'll the neighbours think?'

Dec was great with me. It wasn't the explosive, shouting match-style intervention you may be familiar with from TV. He exhibited no judgment and exerted no pressure; he did the deed with empathy, as maybe only someone who's sat where you're sitting could do.

Dec: How are you feeling, brother?

Me: Desperate. Ashamed. I'm so sorry I've let ye all down again.

Dec: Don't mind us, it's yourself you're hurting the most.

Dec: Do you want to do something about your drinking?

Me: I think so, yeah.

And then I just cried. Sobbed, actually. That was unusual. Normally, I just felt numb immediately after binges. I was told that one option open to me was to go to a drug/drink abuse treatment centre or at least start meeting up with other recovering alcoholics. I'd just got an acting agent, so I felt like a treatment centre was a non-runner. How would I explain to my agent that I was about to disappear for a month? Priorities, like. Also, I wasn't a daily drinker, so I couldn't really see how I needed to be incarcerated to stop drinking.

And then there was the small issue of the fact that I didn't 100 per cent want to stop. In spite of how absolutely desperate I felt at that moment, I knew that in a few days' time the head would start to lift and I'd start missing drink again. I'd go through the entire cycle yet again of initially being sleepless with post-binge depression and anxiety and then being wide awake with anticipation. Because, before long, I'd start excitedly fantasising about the next breakout. I'd open the front door of Charlie's early-morning house after a few weeks of clean living and going to the gym with a new shirt on and all the lads would cheer: 'Aw, yes. Look who's back?' And all the girls would go, 'Oh my God and he looks amazing too!' (This obviously never happened by the way; you'd be lucky to get a grunt or a nod.)

But I thought I'd go chat to some alkies. I didn't see how it could hurt. It would get people off my back and would undoubtedly prove to myself that I was just going through a really bad patch. OK, that patch was kind of going on my whole adult life but the idea that I was a full-blown alcoholic like my mother was absurd.

So, I went to Togher to meet some drunks. It was initially a sobering blow to the majestic ego I'd constructed for myself, which always told me that I'd do it differently. I wouldn't be like the others. I wouldn't fall so low as to need cups of tea and chats with other people who couldn't handle their booze. Shower of losers! But to my undying surprise I really liked the chats. I couldn't get my head around the kindness freely given to me by strangers but I gratefully accepted it. I also noticed they kind of accepted me as I was; I didn't need to put on the usual bullshit act of the carefree party animal. Though great craic, they spoke of 'head stuff' – loneliness, fear – the things I didn't think you were supposed to talk about. Though to start with, I couldn't see the connection between these chats and trying to stop drinking cans.

I didn't understand their kindness then but I've some sense of it now. In those first few months, total strangers offered me more emotional support, empathy and love than maybe I'd ever felt in my life. They offered me practical help and guidance with regard to picking up the pieces with my daughter, access, etc. I was given phone numbers and offers of spare rooms. And I listened to their stories and I saw myself in them, of course I did. I'd even talk about my own drinking story occasionally. I'd leave their company feeling lighter than I'd felt in years, with hope in my heart that there just might be an antidote to the feeling of 'something wrong, something not quite right'.

I'll never forget the first night I sat with a few alcoholics around my age in a since-closed café in Cork aptly named Tribes. My heart was beating so fast because I couldn't quite believe how much we had in common, how we thought similarly, how we felt the same way about ourselves and this strange new life, and we laughed, like a newly released bunch of hostages who had bonded in terror and were now tasting freedom together. I floated home that evening, teary with the exhilaration of having discovered that I still had my tribe, even though I'd left the session.

Looking back on it, there was just one problem: going for tea with other alcoholics started to become just like any other fad, another addiction of sorts, rather than a plan for living or change. And I was still going to pubs. I was a self-anointed saint preaching the good word to the asinine sinners, pulling aside potential problem drinkers and telling them my drink-sodden tales of woe, uninvited: 'It starts off with a few in a respectable place like this but before long, you're selling your mother's heater for cans and waking up naked on a cow shed in Newmarket.'

My ex-drunk Jesus complex didn't seem to be going down too well in the pubs and clubs of Cork, which was annoying. I kinda hoped that when I stopped drinking, the arse would fall out of Cork nightlife generally and that, without their talismanic, self-appointed mascot, the Vintners Association would transition to superfood smoothies. But it seemed Cork was merrily still merry without me.

After about ten months I started to become edgy. I began to focus on the perceived differences between me and other alcoholics I met. I compared myself to them rather than identifying with them and a belief (hope?) that was buried deep inside, but which had always been there, started to come to the surface: I wasn't as bad as these people. *I know I'm wild*, I thought. *I know there are times when I can't stop but there must be a way of controlling it myself. I'm really smart; I just know I can think my way out of this if I really apply myself to it. Also, I'm too young. And finally, I'm too cool. It's unfair of me to simply leave the pubs and clubs and parties of Cork to fend for themselves without me. I have learned so much from these drunks and I am grateful to them, but I'm not done with getting wrecked. I'll give ye a shout in twenty years if you're still alive and brighten up your day.* You might think I'm trying to be funny here but this is an accurate account of my interior monologue in this period. In the end, I didn't make it to one year sober.

Now, this type of absolutely off-the-wall thinking doesn't arrive at the doorstep to your mind as a fully formed package: it gradually seeps in through the vents and windows, it sneaks up on ya. It plays tricks on you. At this time I could go through periods where I would be drinking but still be relatively OK. In 2012 I did the Edinburgh Fringe again in a relatively successful run, drinking a little bit and kind of managing it by putting a series of rules and regulations on myself, which I was more or less able to adhere to. Two pints max after performances, always home in the apartment for a certain time. I did have a small team around me, so it was that little bit easier to stick to the system (the one night I smashed the system and headed off on my own, I got leathered and ended up in a fight about Scottish independence with a lad from Aberdeen. He won both the fight and, as it turned out, the referendum). It never really occurred to me at the time that other people probably don't need a rulebook and a curfew in place to ensure they don't go missing for days on the sauce, but for me it was a massive victory and clear evidence that my time with the alkies had been worthwhile, as they had bizarrely taught me how to handle my booze.

But I wasn't a complete and utter idiot. I could feel something bubbling up inside me that I was eager to ignore but which was undeniable: the feeling that I was making a good job of keeping the lid on the pot but foam was starting to spill out. And then things came to a head.

In 2013 myself, D, B and J went on a weekend to Riga. I didn't draw a sober breath but there was nothing particularly unusual about that. What was new was the recklessness that had started to kick in, not just for me but for others. I found that hard to reconcile with the person I still believed was there, deep inside, who had values and cared deeply for other human beings. I remember a morning in the apartment when I was drunk out of my mind. We were on the top floor of a multi-storey apartment block and I was throwing full cans out the window, not aiming for people but not really caring where they were landing either. Later that day I was caught by a couple of locals pissing on a church wall and they gave me a bit of a beating. Were I sober, I would have hopped on for them. I'd seen English football hooligans do a similar thing in Prague on my Leaving Cert holiday and it disgusted me. I thought it was reprehensible to travel to a foreign country and disrespect their culture and religion in such a manner. I had become everything I detested.

The day we were leaving Riga I was stumbling home in the wee hours, alone, and a woman urged me to follow her into a 24-hour club. I just wanted more drink so gladly obliged. In my simpleton state, she took the card off me, typed in my digits and made the transaction. When I got home, I learned that that pint of Heineken had cost me €650. To be fair, it was very tasty from what I can remember.

In Riga airport, me and my trusty steed D were playing a mash-up of hide-and-go-seek and cops-and-robbers while B and J were staring into space, genuinely quite traumatised after a weekend with Shaun Ryder and Bez. Because the really tasty pint of Heineken had fleeced me, I had to borrow money from J to get myself and D home on the bus from Dublin. But instead of going home, we somehow managed to get into Copper Face Jacks (the iconic Dublin nightclub), me with a black eye and a gash all down the top of my head (I'm not quite sure what condition you'd have to be in to be stopped from entering Coppers). We met a couple of Tipperary girls living in Dublin who probably took pity on us and gave us somewhere to crash.

We were out early the next morning looking for the cure with no money. D momentarily broke – I'd never seen this before. He didn't suffer from my ups and downs at all; I always thought of him as a bit of a machine but, to be fair to him, he'd been drinking to collapse since Thursday. This was now Monday, the rats (DTs) were kicking in and we'd no money to get home. A friend had to drive all the way up to collect us and it was hard to laugh it off in the aftermath. I was in my thirties now and the 'am I or am I not an alcoholic' stage was in the rear-view mirror. I knew well I was an alcoholic with my life spinning out of control. But what was I to do? I'd tried not drinking and it didn't work.

When off on one, I always made sure to have a motley crew around me, plenty of music on the go and generally as much noise as possible to drown out any pesky thoughts like *top yourself*. However, in the last few years of my drinking, a few incidents managed to penetrate the illusion and bring me to my knees in desperation.

One Christmas, a couple of years before my drinking came to an end, I'd been working hard at the 'good boy' routine again but had, without any forewarning, gone on the missing list the afternoon before Christmas Eve. I was sitting in Charlie's early morning house enjoying the festivities when I suddenly realised I was supposed to have Caoimhe just a couple of hours later. On Christmas Eve herself and myself would go into town and hang out, soak up the atmosphere and I'd get her her first present of the season, something she'd pick out on the day, nothing big or extravagant, it was just a little tradition we made for ourselves. Yet again I'd gone out drinking the night before with the intention of having one or two, getting home early blah blah blah. But now it was way too late. (In fact, in later years, I'd come to understand that the moment I had the first drink it was way too late.) I sat by the window in Charlie's and, for some reason, I went up on my knees to peer out the yellow windowpanes to see what the world was up to on Christmas Eve. I instantly wished I hadn't. Across the road was my beautiful little daughter, dressed in her Christmas clothes, holding her mother's hand, looking happy and excited. In a couple of hours her dad would pick her up and she'd get her first Christmas present. Except, he wouldn't. I scurried away from the window for fear of being spotted. In an hour or so, her mother would be forced into some cock-and-bull story to protect our daughter from the truth: that her dad loved going on the piss more than he loved her.

There was also an almost biblical experience in a house I was living in in Douglas Road right before the end. I remember so clearly sitting in the front room listening to Kraftwerk with a few other lads of my own ilk, drinking and drugging on a Tuesday after a bank holiday weekend. I was in my early thirties, unable to work consistently, barely able to pay my way in a cheap-as-chips house share. One of the girls in the house was only just twenty. She was sound and friendly and confident, and when I wasn't drinking we got on like a house on fire. I was in awe of how someone so young was so clear-minded about what they wanted out of life, so unencumbered and responsible. She was just out of college and had a significant role in a big company. She was holding down a relationship, she was driving cars, cooking meals and taking care of herself. This was all well beyond me. I'd make a decent stab at pretending to also be a person like that in front of her but this particular day the jig was up.

She came home from work early and popped her head into the living room where me and the Washed-Up Drunks of Cork Association were having their inauspicious get-together. I'll never forget that head, that day. There was just something in her face that cut through all my bullshit, all my delusions: pity. To me, it was the face of somebody regarding not a party boy but a waster, a dropout, a 'sure God, help us'. I felt shame flush my face and not even blackout drinking could help me escape it. About two days later, when the binge ended, I shook and rattled downstairs to get a drink of water. I walked into the living room only to find that the ceiling had collapsed and entire chunks of it were lying on the sofa, chairs and carpet. I mean, how does that even happen? The house was falling down around me. I'm not sure if you're into the whole 'it's a sign' thing but I started feeling like the end was nigh.

I was a beaten docket; I just didn't realise it at the time. Up until this point I still occasionally took drugs when drinking but on one weekend early 2015 I took Ecstasy for what would turn out to be the last time (I hope). I barely got any kind of high, missed work and prepared myself for the usual two or three days of the depression, self-loathing, 'What are you doing with your life?' kinda lark. But this particular downer didn't go that way. The depression was deeper and the anxiety was like nothing I'd felt since taking snowballs.

I was working with Graffiti at the time, a brilliant theatre for young people in Cork, and was doing a high-energy show for schoolchildren, feeling like I should really be in hospital. In the middle of the run I raided my mother's medicine cabinet and confiscated some Valium and two antidepressants – as in, two tablets. Now, before you fall of your chair laughing or call me a liar, I do actually mean two Lexapro, because for years, after particularly brutal binges, if I felt the depression and anxiety weren't shifting, I'd go to the doctor, he'd prescribe Lexapro, I'd take it for a day or two, start to feel better and discontinue. I'm aware there's no scientific basis for the therapeutic effect (outside a placebo one) but it's what I did and it worked quite well for me.

For most of the following Wednesday I spent the school shows thinking I'd probably have to swing by the local psychiatric unit afterwards to be on the safe side, but by Thursday morning I felt grand. Still, it was a scare. I hadn't felt that low and desperate in years. I thought to myself, *Yokes, by God, we've had a good run. It's time to wish each other well and go our separate ways.*

And that was that: we did. But there was absolutely no thought in my head, even for a moment, of giving up drinking. In spite of the fact that deep down, I knew the writing was on the wall – I knew I was at best a patchy father, a patchy writer and performer, a patchy member of society, really – *I still couldn't bear the thought of a life without drink*. I loved it so much or, at least, felt I needed it so much, that I had accepted my fate as a bit-part participant in life. If I could keep drinking without completely losing my mind, nothing else mattered.

In early May 2015 I went over to London to see my girlfriend at the time. S is a very empathetic person and we've since become good friends, but such was my state of mind at the time that the relationship felt like a battle of wits, a hurt-or-be-hurt, do-or-die. My mood had been shite for a while and I'd gone back to the doctor and got my usual course of Lexapro. Except, this time, a week or nearly two had passed and I didn't have the usual pep in my step. The failsafe wasn't working. Panic.

I was anxious and ruminative, worrying about the potential consequences on Caoimhe of my failings as a father. I also worried about my inability to live with myself if I became one of those hangers-on at parties and nightclubs, one who's too old and delusional to offer anything interesting to the experience. These thoughts and forebodings were swirling around my head as I flew into London to meet a woman with whom I'd become convinced I was in some sort of emotional mortal combat, rather than a relationship founded on mutual caring.

As soon as we met, I immediately played down the significance of me coming over to visit her and immediately got as drunk as I could as quickly as I could in some bar in Walthamstow. Anybody who has ever drunk a lot in the early stages of taking a course of antidepressants will know it's not a good shout. The bizarre sensations of the medication starting to take effect, the physical discomfort and heightened anxiety combined with a barrel of drink is, funnily enough, not a pleasant cocktail. I suppose if I'd been able to sit down and think about things with any semblance of logic I would have spotted something amiss with the plan to drown antidepressants with a depressant.

I always felt like I somehow knew best, though. I fancied myself as the anomaly proving the rule. I decided it would be OK to continue drinking for the next few days. I think in CBT circles they call these 'positive distortions'. They actually serve you quite well when you're a kid experiencing trauma: you imagine that it's not so bad because pretty soon you're almost certainly going to be the lead singer of a famous rock band or the like and everything will be grand. I think all kids have positive distortions, it's what makes them children. I just hadn't grown up.

The morning of 9 May I woke up on a sofa after three days and nights of pass-out drinking in some house with S. She was asleep on another couch. We left promptly and as I went through my pockets, I realised I'd no wallet or keys. My head felt like it was someone else's.

I borrowed some change from S and went into a convenience store to buy a solitary can of Stella. I remember sitting on the edge of the pavement outside the shop unable to converse, slugging on my can, desperately trying to quell the madness, just like when I'd been on the snowballs trip to hell all those years ago.

S was losing patience with me. Why had I come over to visit her if I was just going to silently drink cans on the side of the street? Fair point. Rather than try to put into words what was going on for me, I engineered an argument and left. I walked through the streets of London wondering if people could see the terror behind my eyes and, maybe for one of the first times in my adult life, I realised that whatever was going on in my head, a drink wasn't going to make it better. I felt as if my mind was a tyre and the rubber had almost been fully eroded. The tread was long gone and the unprotected wheel was smashing and sparking off the ground with every thought and move I made. Your whole body is transfixed when you're like that. It's as if at any given moment you're going to be annihilated. The accompanying thoughts (*I've never felt this bad before; this is uncontrollable; I'm going to end up in hospital or dead; what'll happen to my daughter? What'll everyone think? I've done this to myself; I'm worthless; I'm evil; I'm hopeless*) endorse the feeling and then the behaviour gets more and more erratic and now you're drowning in your own mind.

The backdrop to all this was that I was getting my first opportunities with the comedy department at RTÉ and had been making some sketches for them with a view to doing a TV pilot later in the year. With my head absolutely gone fully bananas I checked my phone to find an email from broadcaster John Creedon in my inbox. He was looking for sight or sound of a script I'd promised him days earlier. A thought flashed through my head: *What if I rang him? What if I actually said, 'John, to be honest there, man, I've a wicked drink problem and it's all come to a head in the form of a nervous breakdown. Can we kick that sketch down the road until after I do a stint in hospital?'* He probably would have been really sound about it, knowing him as I do now. I could see him inviting me up to the house for a cup of tea and a chat. But of course, I didn't tell him. I just put it with the other things to worry about – like how on earth I was going to pack my bag, get a tube to the airport and get on a plane back to Ireland in the middle of the worst panic attack of my life.

Somehow, I found myself back in Cork. I made it to my new houseshare in Wilton and a housemate let me in, seeing as I had no keys. I made some excuses and went straight into my room, pulled the blinds and lay on the bed. The terror dialled down just a little bit.

A few days later I felt somewhat OK-ish again. I was able to resume the sketches and start to contextualise or justify what had happened to me in London: it was a weird set of circumstances; the meds were still settling down; it was all S's fault, etc. But in no time at all, the terror returned. What was even more frightening was that, up until this point, I had always believed that if the shit really hit the fan, Lexapro was my panacea. And yet here I was, on it some weeks now, and I felt worse than ever.

Back to the doctor, a few smiles, a few chats about Led Zeppelin and bang: up the dose and I was back on my merry way, assuming that was the problem. I felt good for a few days and then, out of nowhere, I was back to terror, racing thoughts and impending doom. At this point I was moving beyond fear into hopelessness. Something in my brain had broken and no pill could fix me. In a way, I was kind of right.

The doctor upped the dose again but I still didn't feel right. I thought my last chance was to just come off everything. The new theory was that it was all the medication's fault. And so pretty quickly (and when I say quickly, I mean Tadhg quickly – less than a week) I went from 20mg of Lexapro to zero: a titration some people do over the course of several months or years. Within a day or two, I was suicidal.

As I lay in my bed looking at a picture of my daughter, wanting to cry but feeling numb as well as scared and hopeless, I also felt vaguely humiliated. What an unceremonious blow to the ego this was. I reflected on my life. I'd always felt I knew best, that I had the answers for everything, that at any given moment I'd turn it around and go on to achieve the greatness for which I was undoubtedly destined. And yet, Cork's most beloved cheeky chappie, the Marxist leader it never knew it needed, the poet who never wrote, was about to become just another statistic. Gatman fought the gat and the gat won. I couldn't believe it. If I really did have all the answers, if I really did always know best, why was I alone, unable to work, unable to keep friends or girlfriends, and why was I no longer able to manage my own mind? The self-delusion had finally been broken beyond repair. I was torn asunder.

I walked to the A&E unit of Cork University Hospital and told a young psychiatrist that although I desperately didn't want to take my life, I couldn't see how walking around with my head was tenable much longer. I wasn't sure what I was capable of any more. I told him I felt like I must have thought myself into an abyss and, try as I might, I couldn't think my way back out. I was lost in myself. My brain was surely permanently damaged from drink, drugs and emptying battles with this indefinable, all-consuming, fucking fear.

I sat back and waited for him to diagnose some exotic new mental-health condition, presumably for the exceptionally intelligent and cool. Ideally, he would give me a prescription for the corresponding new medication; I would start to feel better and in a few short weeks I'd be in some gaff or pub, telling the lads about my latest wacky escapade. I was in absolute denial that, for the first time, I had presented at a hospital because I feared I would take my life.

Rather than refer to his psychiatric superiors and call a conference on my behalf, he simply asked me if I had any addiction issues. I said I'd struggled with drink and drugs for most of my adult life. He prescribed me something to help me sleep at night and suggested that maybe it was time to give getting sober another go. I begged him to let me stay but I went home, took something called Seroquel, woke up the next day at 2 pm and went through my phone to see if I still had any numbers for sober alkies.

In the last few months of my drinking I reached what for me was a new and final low. One night I had been moping around the Crane Lane bar, drinking my head off, searching for something or someone to take the edge off the loneliness and despair. I was wearing a cheap pair of blue trousers with the arse half ripped out of them. I got talking to this Swiss girl who I hit it off with after she called me a Smurf and attempted to puppeteer me through the rip in the trousers. The Smurfs weren't puppets but no harm done, she was foreign after all. We ended up going back to my place and drinking wine. She was really cool but I started to have this creeping-up-the-back feeling, an aching to be alone. I'd never felt like that before when drinking. I made up some unnecessarily long and elaborate story about needing to be up early or being on antibiotics or some other nonsense and was relieved when she got a cab home. I got into bed, put on *Withnail and I* for the hundredth time, drank two bottles of somebody else's wine and passed out alone. Next time it was cans and

YouTube videos of Ireland World Cup qualifiers but the experience was similar.

The joy of other people was waning. The illusion that I was just having fun at a party had melted away. Now all I wanted was the bottle or the can and oblivion. To my horror, I had become the one thing I most passionately wanted not to be: my mother. In my mind, I could always sell myself the idea that I was just a wild child who went a bit crazy sometimes. Overall, I was one of the good guys, I'd tell myself. I'd achieved in school and college. I was smart. When I was sober, I made everyone else's life just that little bit brighter and better. Any moment now, I'd figure out once and for all how to get a handle on this drinking thing. But now the jig was up. I wasn't that guy. I was my mother, hiding in the shadows from a terrifying, cruel world. Like her, I had opted out. Like her, I had chosen drink over my family.

Although that point was the lowest, loneliest of my life, I did have someone new in my corner. In the run-up to this crisis point I'd met Claire. She was working as a stage manager for a play I was doing in Cork in the summer of 2014. Her first impression of me was that I was cocky, self-seeking and posh. The first two adjectives barely landed a punch but I took absolute exception to the third. She wrongly accused me of being a 'Pres Boy' (Presentation Brothers College, the la-di-da posh school on Mardyke Walk) – which, if you're not familiar with the Cork schooling system, is just about the most insulting thing you can say to a self-anointed working-class hero like myself. She also subsequently told me that she hadn't found me particularly physically appealing, although, from what I can remember, I spent most of that summer practically topless or certainly in a string vest sunning my face and working out furiously in between chaotic drinking binges. That she didn't find me attractive was yet another blow to the fragile ego but naturally made me much more interested in her.

When I first set eyes on her I would have found it hard to believe that we would be friends, let alone become a couple down the line. She seemed like a studious, con-scientious, bespectacled, prefect type (I was actually spot on, she was a class rep in college). She reminded me of the girls who would rat on me when I was cheating on their buddies in nightclubs. She was obscenely organised and literal and not prone to suffering fools or piss artists. Yet we immediately had this life-affirming rapport.

One of the first conversations I remember us having was during rehearsals. I was sitting on the ground dur-ing a break, fiddling with a scooby bracelet my daughter had made for me, saying that when I drank too much, I would look at the bracelet to try to encourage myself to snap out of the session, go to bed and get home in time to see her. To Claire, it was as if I was speaking another language. She found it incomprehensible that somebody would pin their hopes of self-restraint on a bracelet. 'Why don't you just go to bed when you need to? And come home when you're supposed to?' she asked. Christ, girl, if only it were that simple.

Claire was in many ways my opposite but there was something about her, or indeed is something about her, that I hoped, on my best day, with my head clear and my ego in check, I was capable of: kindness. She just always seemed to be in the midst of helping someone or thinking about how she could lighten another's load. She never seemed trapped in her own head and yet she wasn't doing a recovery programme or undergoing any expensive therapy. She often started her day thinking about other people in her life – I usually started my day thinking about me. I was generally unhappy while she was quite literally the happiest person I'd ever met. To this day, she wakes up in the morning with a big smile on her face that seems to say, 'Oh yes, another day of this! How exciting!' I generally wake in the morning pondering the purpose of my existence, reining in my off-the-wall thoughts and desperately trying to interpret my abstract, unnerving dream world that usually involves some deceased parent and portentous words of warning from a rat or a mole.

We'd barely been friends for a few months when I went from this ostensibly gag-laden, cheeky chappie to a guy terrified to leave his room. In the house in Wilton I was looking after a beautiful black Labrador called Inca. I remember one day, probably only a few days away from going to the hospital, turning the key in the door, hot with anxiety, and going into the living room to find that Inca had shat all over the ground. Pathetic fallacy, how are you? My life had literally turned to dog shit.

Claire was terrified of dogs, the only debilitating fear
in her life. The night I came home from the hospital,
at my lowest ebb, I told her I needed to get out of that
house and just go and sleep and chill out in my mam's
for a few days. I also told her that I felt really bad that
there'd be no one to walk Inca. Mam, to her eternal
credit, for all the trauma, for all the fear she lived with
and indoctrinated me with, never once closed the door in
my face. I could quite literally have murdered someone
and she'd take my side, tell me to go up to bed and that
we'd talk about it in the morning. For that, I will always
be grateful.

I certainly wasn't expecting Claire to do anything:
we'd been friends mere months and it was so out of character for me to even share how bad I was feeling with
another human being, let alone someone I'd just met. I'd
become masterful at putting on a front regardless of how
I was feeling. Perhaps it was because I was so desperate
or maybe it was because the connection between us felt
so genuine, but I had completely welcomed her into this
mostly weird, rarely wonderful world. After taking the
Seroquel, which knocked me unconscious for about a
day and a half, I woke up to find that Claire had packed
up my stuff from the house, completely on her own, had
transferred it all to my mother's house, explained the
situation to my landlady delicately and had, most startlingly of all, taken Inca for a walk in my stead. When I
saw my stuff in the front room, I remember thinking to
myself, *If there are people like Claire in the world, it's*

worth me fighting to get back to being happy in it. This extraordinary human being wanted me in her life? Well, that was something. Maybe I wasn't a bad guy, maybe I was just a sick and struggling guy. Claire loved me when I couldn't love myself.

Chapter Ten

Welcome, O Life!

And so I accepted, for the first time in my life, that I couldn't drink or drug successfully. I'd never really been able to. It had always been varying degrees of carnage, and the thing I loved so dearly was slowly but surely killing me. It was only in fear of death itself that I finally loosened my grip and put down the can.

I reached out to sober alcoholics in an entirely different way to how I had the first time, as only the dying know how to. Most importantly, I came back to recovery when the delusions of grandeur finally smashed. If I'd all the answers and knew better than these people, then why was I absolutely fucked and why were they still happy? Psychotherapy, healthy living – these played a part in getting myself right but the only thing that has ever worked to keep me away from booze is other alcoholics. Not even the love and support of my sister, daughter and partner combined could ever keep me dry longer than a few weeks. I tried it. I have to have other alkies and drug addicts. We just seem to understand each other and slowly raise each other from the dead with empathy, honesty and kindness.

If there's one thing I'm certain of in the whole addiction and mental-health racket, it's that there is no one solution that fits all. If you've found your way out of addiction by a means other than a recovery programme and the help of other alcoholics, that's fantastic; as someone who's experienced the hell you've escaped, I'm buzzing for you. For me, hanging around with other sufferers, listening to how they got sober, and learning from them about the pitfalls and triggers was the only thing that helped me to stay stopped.

Some people are opposed to the disease model of recovery – the idea that addiction is an illness we're suffering from that needs treatment. They reckon it disempowers sufferers and stigmatises them. I'm just talking for myself here but rather than stigmatising me, the disease concept offered me relief. Coming back to recovery in 2015, listening to other people's stories, identifying so much with how they felt and thought and behaved, cautiously accepting their kindness, I was overjoyed to come to believe that I, like them, was an alcoholic. I was mentally and spiritually unwell; I wasn't bad or evil. I had worried I was a psychopath or something. How could I possibly be a decent human being if I continued to let people down? How could I prioritise a few cans with the lads over being responsible for my daughter and spending time with her unless I was a narcissist or worse? To find out that I was sick and not bad was revolutionary and seemed to intuitively make sense to me. It constituted hope. It's a bit like the difference between guilt and shame. I can do something about guilt: I've done something wrong and can make amends. Shame makes me feel like the problem is actually me, and not my actions – and that feels like doom.

I'd no problem acknowledging I was sick. I felt it in the churning in the pit of my stomach and if anything, I was sicker when I put the drink down. My thinking was sick. I was completely obsessed with myself, ruminating about the past, panicking about the future, resentful towards the people I had deemed to be inhibiting my path to happiness. But I hadn't realised that I was resentful until I sat down with another alcoholic, who would turn out to be a dear friend and mentor, and truly looked at myself. I thought of myself as this fairly chipper, live-and-let-live type of guy, who was sadly struck down with irregular bouts of melancholia best remedied by a few days of blackout drinking and drug-taking. It was a pinprick to the delusion to realise I was resentful of everyone and everything.

My sister pointed out that if there was a new comedy show on TV, I'd be tutting and groaning before the opening credits had even finished. Everything was 'broad', 'clichéd' and 'lacked balls'. I'd go to see theatre or live comedy and sit there delighted if I thought it wasn't much good, feel better still if the person with me agreed. We'd drink to the cast's misfortune and I'd tell myself and anyone who'd listen that I'd be a star if I only got up there. 'Finally! A nuanced, politically courageous comedian,' they'd say. The problem was that I rarely, if ever, got up there. I did most of my stand-up comedy in Charlie's bar and in drinking sessions around Cork City. My world was small and shrinking. I'd shout jokes and substance-fuelled observations and people would generally laugh. But it wasn't like I was the joy, the giver of life at these get-togethers: the people I drank and drugged with were all funny, our lifestyle was funny, funny things happened to us. I don't think I was the most creative among them but I felt comfortable, that was the thing. That world made sense to me. I was a big bloated fish in a small pond. I was like the kid in school who claims he can do the hundred metres in eight seconds and, when challenged to do it, says, 'Not today, my leg is sore.'

It was all very consistent with the scared little boy who had made up a fantasy life for himself where he was really cool and funny and happy. But self-delusion only works so long. Eventually, it is an ease to have it all smashed before your eyes; the trick is to have the support you desperately need when beginning the process of picking up the pieces.

When people picture a bunch of alcoholics trying to heal themselves they probably think of a cult or Holy Joes. I've been knocking around with alkies on and off now for sixteen years and never once has someone offered me rosary beads or asked me to go to Mass with them. Some still practise their faith, of course, but rarely if ever chat about it or connect it to their recovery from the mental illness that is alcoholism. Most drunks my age and especially younger trying to get sober have no religion at all.

What has been essential to my recovery, which sounds a lot like God but isn't God (I promise), is the concept of a higher power. My perspective on the higher power is effectively: I'm absolutely fucked and I can't run my life any more on willpower, substances are no longer taking the pain of being me away – can something or someone please help me? It may sound like a cop-out but it worked beautifully for me, maybe because I'd always put my trust in powers greater than myself: drink, drugs, the fragile, fit-to-burst ego. I'd no bother trying to seek something deeper, less destructive to pin my hopes on. And for me, it isn't so much what or who I'm reaching out to – it's the reaching out itself, the humility of accepting and behaving like someone who has come to believe they do not have all the answers. It's beautiful, actually. I need help and I welcome it. I feel lighter even writing the sentence. Your higher power can be anything – a deceased relative, the universe. There used be a lad in Cork whose higher power was a bus. Unfortunately my own bus was often late or didn't turn up. So I kept searching for a HP that would work for me.

My breakthrough came in late 2015 when I watched a video featuring Jerry Seinfeld talking about transcendental meditation. He'd been doing it the whole way through filming *Seinfeld* and credited it with assuaging stress and self-doubt. Then I found out that film director David Lynch believes he owed many of his greatest ideas to the 'fishing' that transcendental meditation gave him the rod to do. This was unbelievable. A tool that promised to calm my nutty head *and* make me an iconic artist and world-famous comedian? Oh, baby!

I went to TM teachers in Cork, where I trained in the technique over a few days. It's a mantra-type meditation, meaning you say the mantra silently to yourself during the practice. The mantra itself is meaningless; it's just a short Sanskrit word or sound that merely functions as transport, bringing you to a place of peaceful nothingness. Twenty minutes in the morning, twenty in the afternoon.

I took to it like a duck to Waterford. Almost right away I started to feel a stillness within, a place where my worldly worries and stresses seemed unimportant, where I was not thinking about myself – I wasn't thinking at all, actually; I was just 'being', as they say, and it was pure bliss. I generally come out of a meditation feeling connected to, and compassion for, the people around me who are trying their best, like I am. That's it. That to me is the higher power: that stillness deep inside myself that can be accessed at any time with a quiet room and a meaningless mantra.

For me, if there is a God, it's in me, it's in all of us. I got on better when I stopped looking to the sky and started looking within. There it is, folks, thousands of years of theology condensed into a tea-towel maxim. It's such a pity Thomas Aquinas didn't have me working with him. I would have saved him years of toil. God is within. That's lunch.

So now, I had the love and support of alcoholic strangers – and when I say love and support, I don't mean, 'text if you need anything'. I've had alcoholics at my door in minutes if I told them I was struggling; they've sat with me and walked with me when I needed to spew a load of madness. There's also, as I mentioned, this spiritual principle of giving it away to keep it that underpins everything about people trying to get well after addiction. The people who seem the most well in themselves are generally the ones regularly helping others. They've found a tactic for battling self-obsession that always works.

Alkies and meditation saved my life but I still needed more. I needed to come to terms with my behaviour; I needed to 'clear the wreckage of my past', as they say. I had to take responsibility for my alcoholism and not let myself be a victim. I had to abandon my teenage philosophy, which told me that because I'd been dealt a rough hand, I'd a free pass to treat others as I wished.

So I got myself an alcoholic mentor. A Yoda, if you will. Not that Yoda was on the piss or anything. I digress. A mentor is just like any other alcoholic, except they've usually been around a few years, appear to have found a means of keeping their mad heads calm and they no longer behave destructively, either to themselves or others. In fact, they appear to be really useful members of society. I'd had many mentors along the way who were of immense help to me and offered me friendship, solidarity and understanding, but because I knew my make-up, I understood that I needed to find someone who wouldn't be susceptible to my bullshit. Up until this point, when shortcuts became available, I readily took them, and that hadn't worked for me. In the quest to save my soul and stop myself from either relapsing or becoming danger-ously mentally unwell again, I had to abandon the old one-two of charm and disarm. Instead, I sought out the most brutal, no-nonsense mentor in Cork. The one the others said was too hardcore. I had my man in mind.

When I met him briefly and listened to him speak, I thought to myself, *Whatever it is he has, I want it.* He'd sometimes laugh deeply from somewhere in the depths of himself, this great untethered, booming laugh, like someone who no longer gave a shit what people thought of him (in a really nice way). He was a tree of a man with impossibly large limbs and had been prone to a spot of *Clockwork Orange* ultra-violence in his wild youth. Though bookish, he was also a can-do, practical kind of guy with coal-shovel hands. On paper he was as far removed from me as I could think of, which was bloody perfect. I wasn't looking for a cinema buddy. I didn't just want to hang around with sober alcoholics. I wanted to change. I needed to. I wanted to deal with my head and the hurt I'd caused others – I had to free myself from it.

I'd been working up to asking him to help me take my recovery to the next stage – and popping the question was an ordeal. Well, it was in my crazy head, anyway. I think I would have found it easier to ask him to settle down and rear a family with me. In the end, I got lucky because he asked me. He came up to me one time after a get-together for alkies. He read me the riot act and laid down the guidelines for us working together. I needed to be at his house at quarter to eight on a Thursday or have a very good excuse if I wasn't. I was to exhibit, in my actions not my words, that I was willing to go to any length to get sober, which is very different to getting 'dry'. I'd gotten dry loads of times, I could stop drinking no problem, but up until this point, I wasn't really sober, not emotionally. I hadn't dealt with the resentments, the self-obsession, the self-will run riot – all the stuff that had me drinking my head off to begin with.

Although I was playing it cool to his face, inside I was almost delirious because I knew that life-saving change was now on my horizon, if I could hold my nerve. I told Claire, almost crying with relief, 'D'ya know the big scary fella I was telling you about? He's gonna help me.' And so, every week, I turned up on time. In the early stages I'd be in the middle of bullshitting him a bit and I could just see in his eyes I was wasting both his time and mine, so after a while I just stopped trying to get him to like me. In the nicest possible way, he kind of let me know that it didn't really matter to him if I got it or not. Of course, he'd really like me to get well but that was up to me and the work that I put in. It wasn't going to really put him up or down; he'd been helping people like me for almost twenty years at that stage and if there was one thing he'd learnt in that period, it was that it wasn't about him. It was about the poor little fucker in front of him and their capacity to be honest. And in his front room, week on week, I became more and more honest.

Guided by the Treeman, I'd the opportunity to change, to acknowledge, to confront and move on from my past. I made a list of my resentments from before I drank right up to the present and in writing about them, I tried to understand the ways in which they affected me, what my patterns were – what the things were that triggered me, to use the modern lingo – time and time again. For instance, I had picked up resentments against people and places that I deemed to be unwilling or unable to see my brilliance. I filled copybooks about RTÉ. Do I have legitimate grievances with RTÉ? Yes. Is RTÉ responsible for making me sad and angry? Never. That's my fragile ego, being threatened with annihilation, making me scared and angry, time and time again, year on year. Which brought me to the next part of the writing: what part did I play? Imagine that. All these resentments, all these people and places who'd screwed *me* over throughout the years, and the Treeman expected me to write about *my* part? The cheek. But seeing my part in my problems, the role I played in creating and then nurturing my frustrations with the world, was one of the most transformative things I've ever done in my life.

I made lists of the people I wronged and became willing to make those wrongs right. I told the Treeman everything. I searched the soul and shared all I scavenged, even the unpleasant stuff, the things I thought were so shameful that I couldn't talk about them – until I put them into words and they didn't seem so abominable anymore. More often than not, people were either surprised or happy to hear from me when I'd turn up to make amends. They'd say, 'Well done, boy, you're doing great now. The best amends you can make are to just keep doing what you're doing.' I'd feel ten feet tall after these experiences. It felt like what I'd always hoped confession and penance would do for me when I was a kid but it never seemed to work, because I was only ever talking to a priest rather than the person.

Occasionally, somebody would politely say that they didn't want to hear from me, they didn't wish me ill, but they had no interest or desire to engage. These occasions could be difficult. My egocentric head was prone to creating perfect emotional pre-constructions where I would make my amends beautifully, perhaps cinemati- cally. The person would fall to their knees and say, 'Oh my God, Tadhg, far from being the selfish, ignorant prick that I always thought you were, you're actually a man-angel. I must tell everyone about this straight away and maybe even get an article about it in the *Echo*.'

I obviously wanted to make amends to my daughter but spent a lot of time discussing with the Treeman how to approach it. Because her mother and I had split up so early on, she hadn't directly seen a lot of the worst of my drinking but she was absolutely and undeniably affected by it. It is obviously not a good idea to go into specifics with someone that you're also trying to protect from uncomfortable aspects of your past, especially when, in Caoimhe's case, she was still just a child of thirteen. I'd come to the conclusion that I would just approach it in a general way, and so, one day when I was bringing her home from school, I said, 'Caoimh, there's just something quick I want to say to you before you go.' We leaned against the wall outside her house as I searched for the words. My heart was beating so fast and I felt so overwhelmed, I turned away from her to break the intensity, and asked the ol' higher power to give me a dig out. 'I'm really sorry I wasn't as good a dad as I should have been when I was drinking. I was caught up in myself. But I always loved you very, very much, and I'm here now and I'll always be here, and if there's anything I can do to make it up to you, just let me know.'

As I looked back at her, I was expecting her to be half asleep or already halfway into her house, but instead she was still there, staring at me, crying. Then I started crying. She wrapped her arms around me and she told me she was proud of me, and I told her I was so proud of her and we just stood there holding each other for a bit. And after that, she left. I slowly walked away and thought of my little cherub who was now growing into the wonderful young woman she is today. I thought of her crawling along the floor and up my leg to welcome me home from work. I thought of her getting out of the bed in Galway and marching us back to the beach in the dark. I thought about all the anguish and confusion I experienced trying to get sober and some bit sane. And I thought, it was all worth it. Every beat of it, if only to have had the experience I just had with my little girl.

Chapter Eleven

Ah, You're Not Serious, Another Breakdown?

And next I saw a podium moving towards me, a podium like in the Olympics. With Katie Taylor and Michelle Smith De Brun over in third, joint bronze. Sonia O'Sullivan was in second, silver medal. And I was like, who's gonna be first? And as the podium drew nearer, I suddenly realised – it was my mam. (MUSIC) My mam. But she didn't look like I remembered at all, not drunk or dishevelled or covered in grass or anything. She was pure glamorous with her hair done. She looked beautiful. I goes, 'Mam, you finally got your medal!' She said, 'I did, son, but I want you to have it.' I said, 'Me? Why me, Mam?' And she said, 'Because you've always been my gold medal, son.' And she took the medal off herself and put it on me.'

From 'In One Eye, Out the Other'

So, all was well, really it was. The years in sobriety rolled by and I was infinitely happier and more content than I had been before I'd even started drinking. It was

179

a childlike contentment, like banging a ball against a gate on a hot summer's day with all your mates. I didn't want much. I largely stayed out of conflict with others. I had a higher power in my life that seemed to be guiding me away from my default setting of self-obsession and towards helping other people. And this helping-other-people business didn't come naturally to me. I wasn't my father's son. Before sobriety, my only interest in helping others had been to balance out karma or get a pat on the back. But in recovery, I learnt the pure joy of doing something for someone without it being a big deal or without looking for something in return.

I'm aware I'm not presenting you with a new or radical idea here. 'Give it away and get more back' is so ubiquitous an idea in modern culture (Insta; self-help books) it has almost ceased to have any meaning, but in my humble opinion, it's an undeniable truth and works best when I'm actually doing it as opposed to talking about it. In fact, getting away from myself, escaping the tedious yet incredibly destructive self-obsession was an absolute necessity for me in getting better. I'm not saying doing nice things for yourself is wrong, things like self-care and psychotherapy or meditation, etc. The problem is walking around all day with a head like mine, which, untamed, will think only of my specialist subject: me. Just let me on *Mastermind* now and my knowledge of myself and my grievances, my resentments, worries (about myself) and ambition will absolutely blow you away.

Thinking is another addiction and, very much like drinking and drugging, it's great craic at the start. You place yourself in all sorts of fantastical scenarios, cast yourself as the hero of every narrative – in my case, a kind of mash-up of Karl Marx and Rambo: a brilliant philosopher-equaliser going around righting personal wrongs and cleaning up the mean streets of Cork City. But then it seems to turn on you. The fantasies wear thin and the stories become darker, self-injurious. And, unlike drink and drugs, it can seem like you're unable to 'stop' your head.

The uncomfortable truth about alcoholism and mental illness, in my experience, is that it's solipsist. Alcoholism is 'me-ism'. The sheer beauty of recovery is that not only does it offer you a route out of living in your head, it facilitates long-overdue accountability and a clearing of the wreckage of the past. Though I had a challenging childhood, and perhaps a genetic predisposition to alcoholism and anxiety, the facts on the ground are still that I treated people like utter shit and I must accept full responsibility for that and make good where possible in order to have any chance of getting well. I went nowhere as long as I continued to blame my mother for every little or large thing that went wrong in my life.

So, I was a free man. My meet-ups with other alcoholics had begun to slowly evolve and increasingly I was helping as much as I was helped. I became a mentor myself. Claire and I went from being friends to starting a relationship and before long we were living together. My lifelong dream of making TV comedy was starting to come true as I began to further develop my relationship with RTÉ, and they somehow gave me responsibility to write, direct and play the lead role in a sitcom for them. More importantly, my family stopped worrying about me and my relationships with them, and with old and new friends, took on a completely new character. It was almost too good.

The first indication that something was awry, even though of course I didn't see it that way at the time, was that work had started to become an obsession. From doing the RTÉ sitcom right through to churning out sketches on Twitter that would sometimes end up on BBC and incur death threats, the way in which I was working was unhealthy. I was no longer motivated by a reasonable ambition to do well, provide for my family and get my work out there. I'd started to feel a resumption of that uncomfortableness within, an indecipherable inner critic shitting on any little win, highlighting all the things I should have achieved. I felt like a horse at the Grand National with the lad on my back I thought was my buddy now whipping me to ribbons.

I suppose if you have the belief from childhood that you're not good enough, it creates a void. My experience was that I needed to stay very close to the spiritual path in order for the void to be filled, especially if drink and drugs were no longer an option. And yet I started to deviate from the spiritual path. Meeting up with other alkies started to become less frequent, contact with the Treeman started to wane, personal accountability didn't seem as important anymore. But in my head, it was all grand. A kind of spiritual arrogance had started to take hold. I was on radio and television talking about my alcoholism journey. I was a survivor, I had beaten it. I was helping young fellas get well, I'd a meditation practice. I felt I was invincible.

Recently, I was listening to an alcoholic sharing his story on YouTube. He said he got into trouble somewhere along the line when he started to believe that it was he himself who had turned his life around, not a higher power or the help of other alcoholics. I nearly fell off my chair. That's exactly what happened to me. 'Me-ism' had started to kick back in. I'd got myself well. I'd had this awful childhood, then I had all these addictions and mental-health difficulties, but look at me now, baby! Now I'm touring Ireland and Britain; I'm marching towards C-list celebrity status in Cork, Belfast, Glasgow and, arguably, Cardiff.

And the me-ism had a dangerous ally: pride. I loved the idea of myself as this healed, spiritually accomplished individual, especially with regard to my family. I used to be the fuck-up, I was the one they worried about, but now I was a celebrity mystic and I'd never have another problem again, the end. And I certainly wasn't about to tell anybody about my little secret. Magic mushrooms. I used to play in an 80s music double act with the absolutely inspired name 'The GR80s'. Me and my buddy, C, had a hilarious tempestuous relationship and would often have disagreements and little scraps on stage. I love him to bits and our wayward banter used to help with the sometimes boredom, sometimes outright terror of playing camp 1980s music in rough little pubs around Cork City and county. In the summer of 2019 another musician friend had told me about how he'd started microdosing magic mushrooms to aid his creativity and had said that it gave him a few giggles and waves of euphoria during gigs. 'Giggles' and 'waves of euphoria'? Keep talking.

Mushrooms had always occupied a grey area in my mind. During difficult periods of drinking and drug-taking, I'd taken psilocybin and experienced nothing like what I'd ever experienced on any other substance. You don't really get a profound sense of God and a moving connectedness with all living organisms off a bag of coke or a line of speed. In fact, I often felt like mushrooms were steering me away from drink and other drugs. After trips I'd sometimes go weeks without drinking or using again. Maybe because I had been gifted a glimpse of that connectedness I had always been searching for. The desire to get off my head and pollute my body would temporarily disappear and I'd find myself stopping to admire trees in Fitzgerald's Park. (Though obviously, after a while, I got bored of staring at trees and would pick up a drink again and get back on the not-so merry-go-round.)

I told myself that these days, there'd be no hassle with a few little naturally-growing-in-the-ground mushrooms. Sure, I was a mystic! Those lads always seemed to have some sort of herb or plant on the go, what harm could a microdose do anyway? I was after taking macrodoses of everything else. And now another crucial tenet of my recovery seemed to be making its way out the window: honesty. I started taking the odd microdose/not-so-micro dose at GR80s gigs and was having a great time, but do you think I mentioned it to anyone? Not a hope. How could I? Mystic Tadhg, the lord, the giver of sober life around Cork, could hardly let the young fellas he was helping out know that he'd started dabbling with a class-A drug. They mightn't understand that it was purely for spiritual reasons and not some latent ancient desire to still be getting a little bit wrecked every now and then. Not on your nelly. In my mind, I was now not only the most healed alcoholic in Cork, I was also more healed and enlightened than regular people who had no trauma whatsoever.

Before long I found myself walking through forests with a couple of good buddies taking full doses of mushrooms, laughing our heads off, having beautiful, profound epiphanies. On one occasion we were walking through Ballyhoura woods and it suddenly hit me that I wasn't that important – in a good way. I was literally stopped in my tracks by the sheer, spectacular truth of it. All this pressure I didn't even know was there seemed to melt away. I lifted my head and bellowed at the lads: 'Guys, I'm not that important!' The two lads had already walked ahead and weren't even listening to me. Absolutely perfect.

But then, in time, I started taking a little bit on a random Saturday walking through town. At this stage I kind of knew, deep down inside, that something was wrong. The aid-to-spiritual-growth theory was wearing thin. The most obvious indication that I'd flown too close to the sun should have been when the full trips ceased to be enjoyable. I had also started using them as a way of escaping the self-created work stress I was under. I should have known then what I know now: when it comes to substances of any kind, I simply can't have nice things. There is a more-ishness, which kicks in sooner or later, that I just can't control. Be it the most godly plant or powder known to man, if I find it and like it, I'll have to stuff it into my body until I feel like I'm going to vomit it all back out, or die, or both. That's me, kids. You enjoy yourselves though, yeah?

At the beginning of 2022, on paper, things were just dandy. I had more work than I could literally manage. Claire and I were getting on great, as were myself and the daughter. And yet I felt off. The happy, joyous and free state of mind I'd discovered after working with the Treeman was a distant memory. Instead, I was ratty, due in no small way to petty, pseudo-intellectual squabbles I'd often get myself into on Twitter. As I have you there, in my humble opinion, if you want to keep your mental health healthy, rebuff the seductive advances of a social media spat or even generally engaging with faceless multi-digits who call you names. It mightn't upset you too much the first few times someone calls you a 'Marxist, terrorist-supporting scumbag' but if you're reading through an avalanche on a daily basis, it eventually has to take some sort of a toll.

Now, don't you go getting me wrong. I'm not complaining for a moment. I'm a big boy and I'm only too aware of how provocative some of the sketches I put out can be; in fact, that's partly why I make them. But in hindsight, a healthier approach might have been to post the sketch and let people alone to decide if they enjoyed it or not. Instead, I was actively engaging with almost every criticism, cataloguing and responding to every bucket of shit thrown at me. Luxuriating in it. Loving it until, just like every other addiction, it seemed to stop loving me.

The work I was doing had also now begun to lose its vim. I had taken on a podcast, which afforded me the opportunity to meet many high-profile politicians and journalists I greatly admired, like James O'Brien, Gerry Adams and Plaid Cymru MP Liz Saville Roberts. But as I listened back to interview recordings, I became stupefied with self-doubt. I came across as timid and my questions seemed uninspired. I had intended to create a podcast with episodes based on specific topics relating to Brexit and, in particular, the north of Ireland, Irish unity, Scottish independence, the threat of a return to violence, etc. with contributions from my arsenal of high-profile interviewees, all done, of course, in an irreverent and at times thigh-slappingly hilarious way. But I found myself out of my depth. My editing skills were shite and I wouldn't let anyone else at it because I'm a creative control freak. Instead, I wandered into a straight-up weekly interview model. Absolutely nothing wrong with that but though my guests to a man and woman were superb, I felt like I'd let them down and the overall quality of the podcast to me was lacklustre.

I started to question why I was doing it in the first place. I certainly had no passion for podcasting. Maybe I'd taken it on because someone asked me to. I was flattered. Plus, asking a range of politicians and journalists to contribute and most of them replying in the affirmative was nice for my gnawing need for approval, which was back with a bang. But I felt like a bit of a fraud. My passion was, and I'd imagine always will be, creating original and hopefully subversive comedy for stage and screen; not doing it to be liked or be famous but just to make the work itself because it's buzzing around my head, and it's better for me and the people around me that it gets out and gets on with its own life. I recently heard the wonderful Booker Prize-nominated author Claire Keegan respond to a question put to her on RTÉ about how much her recent success would boost her career. She replied, 'I don't have a career. If I was a career woman, I'd probably tried to have gotten a job in the UN. I think to be an artist is to go against what is career thinking and go off and get lost and hopefully get lucky, as I did, and find some readers.' I like that. I identify with that. I aspire to that.

But the podcast and a few other gigs I'd taken in around that time seemed inauthentic to me then. At the risk of sounding ungrateful or arrogant, I don't really enjoy doing the 'mad fecker/ comedy man' interview slots on national radio. You know the ones where they say: 'Tadhg, you big mad fecker ya, say or do something funny there now and give us all a much-needed giggle – but for God's sake just don't mention the housing crisis.' I'm no good at those. My jokes are all wrong. I've genuinely emailed producers asking them not to have me on again on the very rare occasion they might want to. And yet, in this period, I couldn't get enough of 'comedy man haha' slots. I think I'd started to want to be famous again. The void was back and the voice in the head, raucous: *You're not good enough.*

By December 2021 I was locked in a little room at home working bananas hours, rarely meditating, taking no exercise, having no contact with alcoholics, seeing no one, really, other than Claire and Caoimhe. In this period I actually began to consider the possibility of living my life without any friends. I was so consumed with work that I began to see friends as taking up an awful lot of time – texting, ringing, asking them how they are, going for coffee and walks, 'hanging out'? That's a lot of wasted hours that could be put into driving me forward to some unspecified place with a work-in-progress title of 'successful'. In short, I had gone quite mad.

I'd been feeling like a little bag of shit for some time but had been ignoring it. *I'll just ramp back up the meditation and I'll be grand.* Before I got a chance to, in the middle of the night, I woke with a pain in my stomach that can only be described as the worst pain in the history of the world. I had to wake up poor Claire, who absolutely loves her kip. Tired or not, though, she's an out-and-out ninja in a crisis. We both thought it might be appendicitis, as the pain was ludicrous, and she drove me straight to A&E. I fell in the door and in a matter of minutes was in a cubicle with a nurse who immediately prescribed me a painkiller suppository. There followed a moment I thought I'd take to my grave but have decided to share with you for some reason: blinded and unreasonable with pain, I unfortunately got a little sick on the poor girl's leg as she bent me over a table and lodged that sweet, sweet morphine up my 'how you gettin' on yourself?'.

It turned out to be a brutal case of kidney stones and one of the highlights of the experience was another nurse telling me that the pain is supposed to be as bad as giving birth. My God, I got a few weeks out of that one. Every woman I met was put back in her box in no uncertain terms. 'I've felt your pain!'

Lying on the trolley absolutely out of my box on morphine, I thought the worst had passed. The following Saturday, however, I was at home when I woke up and I just felt really panicky, like the bad-old-days panicky. I found this extremely difficult to accept. I'm enlightened now, mystic Tadhg, etc. *I just need to get up and get on with it*, I told myself. The next day, I got a bus to Dublin to join the Save Moore Street protests and when I got off, I felt terrified. Suddenly, walking to Moore Street and chatting to fellow protestors seemed like the most arduous task I could imagine. I was in the midst of a full-on panic attack, the likes of which I hadn't experienced since the drug-taking days. What the fuck was going on?

I somehow managed to get through the protest and get back on the bus. I calmed down a little bit but the next day this disturbing, recurring thought started to loom large in my mind. *What would happen if you snapped again? You're self-employed. How are you going to provide for your family if you can't work?* Followed closely by, *What if this snap is the snap? And all your family and friends and everyone who thinks that you're healed finds out you're the fuck-up again?*

I didn't sleep that night or the following night. By the Tuesday of that week, I was deranged. I was forced to do something I hadn't done since my drinking and drugging days: cancel work. I grew up in a household and community that seemed to use this as the clearest barometer for whether somebody had a substance abuse or mental health issue. You could be as mad as a box of frogs or drunk as an alien seven nights a week, but once you were going to work you were 'grand'. I carried that barometer and shame of being 'work-shy' into my adult life. I was so frightened and demoralised about missing more work that, despite having almost seven years of really good recovery and having a strong meditation practice, instead of leaning on the spiritual stuff, I rang the doctor looking for drugs.

I'll pause briefly for a confession. When I thought I was through the worst of this meltdown, I made a video which went kinda viral, hawking the philosopher Alain de Botton's paradigm shift of breakthrough rather than breakdown (the actual breakdown itself, in de Botton's words, is 'not merely a random piece of madness or malfunction; it is a very real – albeit very inarticulate – bid for health'. The body, unable to get your attention with subtle hints, now starts screaming at ya and kicking your head in, which is exactly what happened to me) and listing some of my top tips for mental-health recovery, including exercise and spending time with friends, etc. I made the video with good intentions but it wasn't completely honest. Part of my recovery also involved taking antidepressants. I consciously left this out. I omitted it because of shame. I felt like the pharmaceutical option didn't quite fit with the cured-mystic persona and, in hindsight, I realise that I was still hanging onto this idea of myself as somehow beyond needing help and support, pharmacological or otherwise.

Shortly afterwards, I watched a performance of Pat Kinevane's stunning one-man show *Silent*, about homelessness and mental illness. During the performance, he broke the fourth wall and asked the audience if anyone had taken, or was now taking, antidepressants. Five or six people put up their hands in a room of about five or six hundred. Obviously, statistically speaking, this just couldn't be accurate. Kinevane heaped praise on the brave few. I sat there feeling hot with shame and knew it was a wrong that would have to be righted.

So I'm sorry I didn't include it in the video. If even one person had got something out of hearing that I needed running, meditation AND some medication to bounce back then it was a missed opportunity. I am sorry to have succumbed to self-created pressure to avoid public acknowledgement of taking medication for fear of looking weak. The real weakness is in bullshitting people. The first and foremost aim of the game is to stay alive. If medication helps you to do that, that's just wonderful.

The doctor prescribed me Lustral and that old put-a-horse-to-sleep tab called Seroquel. A short course of these in 2015 had worked a treat. Back then, transcendental meditation and working with the Treeman had had me tablet-free in a matter of months. This time, however, they weren't cutting the mustard. To be fair to Seroquel, it was still knocking me out but my mood remained, on and off, pretty poor. It was uncannily like the Lexapro experience and it really felt to me that, just like back then, a deeper, more spiritual solution was required than a few tablets and off you go back putting your wigs on and making sketches in your garden.

Three months down the road and I was still very up and down. I was playing the performance of a lifetime at home with Claire, pretending I was tickety-boo and preparing for a national tour, and yet spending more time than not questioning my sanity and trying to come up with new methods to quell the overwhelming agitation. I weaned myself off the medication with initial good results. For a few weeks I felt close to myself again. I started to think of the period as just a blip that I could put down to the attack on the serotonin resources caused by the magic mushrooms, which were undeniably a factor, but there was much more to it than that. Before long I was anxious and low again, and that old, unmistakable, all-consuming childhood fear was there or thereabouts in everything I did, thought and felt. It must have been so difficult for Claire but she never showed it. Again, because she's some sort of a socio-spiritual Wonder Woman, she never really bombarded me with 'are you OK?'s. She very, very gently suggested we do things to make me feel better without ever pressuring me, she left me alone without ever leaving me on my own and, for the second time, saved my life just by being her.

In May and June 2022 I found myself touring around the UK with a one-man show about mental illness, ironically perhaps the most mentally unwell I'd ever felt in my life. I was worse than ever because I almost couldn't believe and certainly couldn't accept that I was somehow back in this torture chamber again. My days during that period consisted of walking long distances to take the edge off suffocating agitation, meditating sometimes four or five times a day to try and get it together for work tasks like live shows, and then simply praying and over-exercising in the hope of getting some sleep – more often than not, my prayers weren't answered. In this period of near-hopelessness I had sell-out shows in London, Belfast and Glasgow, did live TV and radio and made many other public appearances, including the Blindboy podcast to a sold-out Cork Opera House. It's truly incredible to think of what's potentially going on behind the forehead of an apparently fully functional member of society.

By the start of June I was back in Ireland and doing a couple of homecoming gigs in the Everyman, in Cork. The packed room was composed of many family and close friends, and Claire told me afterwards that she'd scarcely ever felt such love in a room as she did that last night. There was a standing ovation from the audience but I felt like I was looking at myself just as they were. I felt detached, watching somebody else going through the motions.

After the run finished and after several more sleepless nights, I got out of my bed one morning unable even to walk or run off the agitation to proceed with the 'I'm grand' routine for Claire. Even the most straightforward tasks, like getting out of my clothes and into the shower, seemed insurmountable and, in any case, pointless. I hadn't known it was possible to feel this combination of terrified by and yet somehow indifferent to the world and my participation in-it. Then throw that element of bruised ego into the equation. This had become perhaps the greatest mystery the mystic had ever witnessed. I had done all the right things; I thought I had created buttresses for myself, protective guarantees for wellbeing and yet here I was again, desperately not wanting to die but absolutely out of ideas as to how it was possible to live.

Let's call a spade a spade. In spite of what Instagram might tell you, when you're truly mentally unwell, a session of hot yoga and a bag of kale may not turn that frown upside down. The first thing I did was go back to the doctor to start another antidepressant. I knew tablets weren't the answer in themselves, but they might just provide a waterproof coat as I went out into the wild searching for it. First things first: survive.

I knew I was going to have to dig deep and that the pills were only the beginning and not the end of the healing. Maybe for the first time in my stupid little life (jokes, I love my life!), I was going to have to confront the fear that had been operating surveillance on me since day dot. I tried to commit to paper the experience of what I was feeling. I knew I couldn't heal myself on my own but I at least wanted to be armed with something a little bit more tangible than 'I feel shit' when I would sit down with a therapist.

The medication gave me just enough pockets of manageability to allow me to effectively describe to myself the depressive/anxious state as I experienced it. I wrote that fear popped up usually in response to some event and, for all intents and purposes, it might as well be that same childhood terror because the sensations were identical to those I'd experienced when I was a kid: churning in the stomach, sweat on the forehead, unpleasant electric pulsations on the skin, head aching and the perception that the brain or head is going to explode. I didn't know what this fear was or what it wanted from me or when it was going to dissipate. Frightened, self-flagellating thoughts descended and spiralled, quickly taking me to that place of annihilation. It took me to the point where social/productive activity was almost non-existent, I spent more and more time alone and my thoughts and feelings settled down into a negative feedback loop. You wouldn't need to be Carl Jung or even Dr Phil to conclude that finally confronting this fear was the only thing for it.

On and off, for most of this period, Mam had been on my mind. I went back to a night when I'd gone to the Treeman's house with a dossier on the injustices done to me by my mother, hoping he'd have open ears and arms and tell me how sorry he felt for me. In actual fact, he effectively told me to get over it, that we were here to look at me and my behaviour, not hers, and that I should get on with the business of making amends to the many people I'd hurt. Harsh but exactly what I needed in that period. I had to clear my own wreckage before I looked at anyone else's. But now something deep inside myself was screaming that I needed to not just make amends for my selfish, insane behaviour towards others, I also needed to confront and understand some of the contributing factors which helped make me fearful to begin with. I had to do the unthinkable. I had to go and spend some time with Mam.

For this trip down memory cul-de-sac, I needed a guide and a helping hand. I was blessed to find myself a psychotherapist who, weirdly, kind of reminded me of my mother. Specifically, the parts of her I loved: the humour, the quaint-but-colourful Cork phraseology and the directness. Using a method I think I recognised from the ol' philosophy degree, she seemed to help me to help myself. Socrates, innit? Bubbsie allowed me to talk, and made me feel heard and understood. She helped me to take honest, sober stock of my childhood for the first time. It was a relief. A lifetime of avoiding feelings had come to an end. And the pain, though brutal, was infinitely preferable to the discomfort of sitting on it and trying to protect it from yourself and the world.

Bubbsie introduced me to the concept of the inner child: a cliché to you potentially, a staggering bolt of awareness for me. I finally had some context for this extreme childlike terror, which had cast itself in my life as an unwanted, often central character. It was something that seemed so obvious in hindsight but before psychotherapy, I couldn't name it. It explained why what was happening now and back then felt the same. The lost, scared little boy had never been comforted and validated so he came searching for reassurance from me at the most inopportune times. The 'inner child' concept explained my workaholism, my obsession with being loved and with pats on the back, with being told I'm a good boy. All that stuff stemmed from a childhood fear of not being enough, of not being mentally strong enough or funny enough to soothe my mother when her 'nerves were at her', to use her own words. The 'inner child' perhaps even shed light on why I'd become a comedian in the first place. Regardless, one thing was certain: his fear was my fear. There was little to no difference in the sensations in my body and mind when I was having the freak-out at the Moore Street demo than when I was back as a little boy in the toilet trying to find a way to articulate to my mother that my head was about to explode.

I went back into the mindset of that little boy and felt again the sensations and feelings of the burden of trying to soothe not myself but my mother. I ached to make her fears and phobias disappear; I hid my own difficulties for fear of worsening hers. I pretended I was permanently OK and had all the answers. I realised where the mystic fantasy had come from. And Bubbsie made me see just what a colossal burden it was to pretend to be perfect all the time, the amount of effort that that entailed. I felt I didn't have to pretend anymore. And though I saw just how directly my mother's issues had affected me, strangely I came to accept and love her more. She was a balm-pot; I'm a balm-pot. Yet she had no recovery, meditation or psychotherapy to help her. She had Valium and booze and rosary beads and she got sicker and sicker. She didn't set out to make me fearful, she was too consumed with her own terror to bother. It wasn't her fault and it wasn't mine either. But it was my responsibility to finally work at letting it go, for me and my family. And it was also my responsibility to actually let Mam go, to grieve her, because only a few months after I had my last drink (I hope), my mother passed away.

I told Bubbsie about the day she died. One morning, late in 2016, I was lying in my old childhood bedroom. I wasn't long sober and was between rented gaffs, and Mam, as she always did, had offered the temporary bed and board, no questions asked. She had a wonderful home help who'd come a few days a week and give her a hand with bathing and the like. My mother wasn't an old woman by today's standards, only in her mid-seventies, but her inability or unwillingness to put up even a perfunctory fight against arthritis had ravaged her limbs and rendered her bed- and armchair-bound, in a lot of pain and on a lot of medication. I heard the home help downstairs in the room Mam was now sleeping in. There was uncharacteristically no chat. I knew instantly that my mother was dead.

I had spent so many years dissociating that I had built up a resilience to traumatic events: I could calmly, intellectually accept them but perhaps not feel them. To feel was to be overwhelmed.

I walked downstairs and into my mother's room, felt her face and noted that she was cold to the touch. It seemed that she had passed away peacefully in her sleep, presumably of heart failure, which was confirmed later by the doctor. As I looked at her, I started to think that I should feel sad now, that I should break down, wail. I should do all the things I didn't do when my dad died to avoid the excruciating delayed reaction. But I couldn't. I couldn't contrive it.

My sister and brothers were on the scene in no time, as was the unnecessary ambulance. I played the role of a son grieving for his mother as authentically as I could, but I felt nothing. It's a horribly cold thing to say, I know, but when you train yourself well enough to feel nothing that's exactly what you're going to get. My brothers and I sat round her bed telling stories, laughing and joking. My sister was momentarily horrified, as if we were in some way blaspheming against the fallen deity, because that's the kind of power my mother had over us. We all felt it and rejected it, and then felt it twice as bad when it came back. Maybe me and my brothers dared to blaspheme because God was dead, or maybe we'd all just dealt with the pain and trauma of having a mother who was never really emotionally available by making ourselves largely emotionally unavailable to her in life as well as, bizarrely, in death.

That night, after her body was removed for preparation for the funeral, I stayed in her house again, as did my sister. I lay in my room in the dark taking in the enormity of her passing. Remembering nights sitting by her side after falls, thinking of the symbolism of it all, my mother the obstacle, literally and figuratively lying in my path to the front door. But now the path was clear. She was gone. And I certainly didn't feel happy; I felt a bit lost. I tried to get my head round the significance of having no living parent in the world and then I quickly pushed that thought out because I didn't want to run the risk of feeling.

I remember clicking into YouTube trying to find some music to distract me. I can't remember what I put on, but the very next song was 'Asleep' by the Smiths. I vaguely knew the tune and had always thought it beautiful, but had never really fully heard the words. Once, a lecturer in college had told us that he stopped listening to music altogether because it would bring up too many emotions. Now I understood. Morrissey's reflections on wanting to be sung to sleep and being content to not wake up any more tore me asunder.

I started sobbing. The kind of crying a kid does when their lower jaw starts quivering and they just can't stop. I think the last time I sobbed inconsolably before that was when Italy knocked us out of the World Cup back in 1990. I went downstairs and I replayed the song for my sister who was washing up alone in the kitchen. We held each other and cried together as we had fourteen years earlier in Cork airport when I left for Edinburgh for the first time. It felt good to feel.

The following night when no one was around, I sat with her in the funeral home. The first thing I noticed was how beautiful she looked. She didn't wear make-up often. For the last fifteen years or so of her life, she never really went anywhere and the make-up now reminded me of the glamorous, charismatic woman she once was. I felt proud of her – something I had rarely, if ever, experienced before. I thought to myself, *You have to hand it to her, they are exquisite cheekbones.* I proceeded to have easily the best conversation with her I ever had – granted, I was mentally playing the role of her replies but still it was a soothing and really quite beautiful experience. I told her I was sorry for all the hurt and worry I'd caused her with my own addiction. I told her I understood that she tried her best and was battling her own demons and trauma, and I told her I loved her. And I knew she loved me in her own absolutely off-the-wall way. I kissed her on the head, walked out the door and tried to get my head around a life and a world without Mam.

As I spoke to Bubbsie about her, she'd be in the back of my head screaming: 'Jesus Christ, you're disgracing me! I wasn't that bad at all.' She was worse but, at times and in ways, she was also brilliant and oozing with charm. This was something Bubbsie picked up on very early, something I seemed to have totally lost touch with: for all the resentments and frustrations I had with the woman, I loved her. I might have just told some harrowing story about picking her up off the floor or something, but Bubbsie would often see something I missed behind the telling.

Bubbsie: You loved her though, did you?

Me: Do you reckon?

Bubbsie: Well, you often smile or even laugh when you talk about her.

(A beat.)

Me: Wow, yeah, I do, don't I?

By casting my mother as the devil and my father as God, I was only reinforcing the Manichaean mindset I was supposedly trying to escape from. And it inhibited healing. By painting her as an unredeemable baddie, I missed the whole point, the whole source of my pain. She wasn't a baddie, she was just sick like me, and it hurt like hell that though there was a great person in there, I couldn't seem to reach her or draw her out too often. I remember crying during a session one time and being assured that I was probably finally grieving.

Me: But what exactly am I grieving? What's the loss? As far back as I can remember, I didn't so much as have a solitary calm and sane conversation with her.

Bubbsie: Maybe you're grieving the relationship you didn't have? The one you always wanted?

I nearly fell off the couch. That was it in a nutshell.

There's not a time goes by when I'm playing a female character and the make-up artist says, 'Oh my God, you look great as a woman, it must be your high cheekbones,' that I don't smile to myself. Mam was my first audience and she was incredibly demanding. I felt the responsibility and pressure to make her laugh, which probably kick-started a fairly useful preoccupation with crowd-pleasing. Her roguish charms and this mysterious ability to get other people to do her bidding are things that I've either consciously or subconsciously inherited myself.

In therapy, I remembered occasions when I'd be with her doing the shopping in town. I'd be in the newsagent's flicking through a copy of *Match* magazine. She'd have one eye on me, of course, perennially worried for my safety, but she'd also be chatting to the staff in the shopping centre, trying to get them to give her a deal or luring them into gossiping about their co-workers. She was vibrant and mischievous and I could see the staff got a kick out of her, and that made me happy and proud. It was like in those moments she forgot to be frightened. If you could have somehow taken away her fear, you'd have had a completely different person, probably quite a fabulous one. I'd have had a completely different mother. I would've given anything to take her fear away.

I'll never forget visiting her in hospital just a few years before she passed away. To us, she had become this charmless, burdensome fixture in the house that caused us all great pain and often had us reluctantly competing with each other for her twisted approval. I walked into her ward to find her hospital room mates enraptured by my mother as she told some story about her charming a furniture guy into giving her a free armchair and a couple of footstools. They were on the edge of their beds, mesmerised by my mother's exuberance and comic timing. It was like watching a different woman. I suppose I *was* watching a different woman. Maybe we were as bad for her as she was for us. But as I watched her there, hogging the room, shouting out the stories, braggin', making everyone laugh, I realised that, much as I wanted to be, I wasn't very much like my dad; I was my mother's son, warts and all.

Now, in the therapist's room, I knew I was scared and was fairly sure where it had come from. If you've had fear all your life, letting it go is in some ways daunting. I'd always been scared and in many ways my lifestyle, my personality, my career choices were all geared towards convincing myself and the world that I wasn't. This is another attractive utility of drink and drugs. When I was off my game, I was fearless; I'd fight the biggest fella in the room even though I wasn't worth a slap (Corkish for shit at fighting). I could see very clearly now that I was run by fear. It was time to take the hugely painful but absolutely necessary step of stopping running and slowly turning around to face my tormentor.

To my great surprise, I discovered that there was nothing there. It was a phantom. I had taken the fear baton from my mother, no questions asked, and run like hell, without considering the destination. That is not to say that the fear wasn't real. The feelings were the realest thing I'd ever experienced. It's just that when I stripped it all back and ripped to the root, my primary fear was of fear itself. If fear crept in, the facade of the healed and happy-go-lucky mystic began to creak.

Psychotherapy helped me to start thinking about my issues in a very practical way, another Copernican revolution, which really worked for me. I had always thought of my head as this mysterious entity, which at times I simply had to obey rather than challenge or, God forbid, understand. I thought of myself as an exceedingly brilliant man of the Friedrich Nietzsche ilk. I feared that one day, like Nietzsche, I'd witness a few horses being mistreated and drop to my knees in neurotic solidarity and descend into madness, never to return (I'd always imagined that the Grand Parade facing out towards the old Fás building would be a good location for this scene). So when I felt off, I almost had the sensation of throwing my arms up in the air and saying, 'I don't know what's going on in my head right now, maybe I'll just go for a run and hope that my head will leave me alone sooner rather than later.' The psychotherapy empowered me to realise that I didn't have to be a slave to my feelings and thoughts anymore. I think that was the single best bit of news I received during breakdown the third.

I was starting to feel much better. I had perspective on my childhood, I had faced my fears and I had started to feel more in control. But I still had crazy thoughts and I still had the propensity to believe them. The only thing psychotherapy lacked, and this is just my experience,

were practicable, effective tools at managing the spiral-
ling thinking that always precipitated the anxious and
depressed feelings. Because I'm an all-or-nothing type
of guy, I said to myself, now that I've opened the door
marked 'help', I might as well keep going to see if I can
tackle the thinking once and for all. CBT had been suggested to me so many times over the years it had ceased to
have any meaning in my mind. People told me that it was
a great aid to managing or redirecting your thoughts. But
I had always been in denial that I had a thinking problem.
Ceteris paribus, my self-talk was pretty good. (Nah, I'm
being coy here: it was unreal.)

During an early CBT session, the counsellor discussed
negative distortions – a cornerstone of the modality. There
are at least ten negative distortions that are very common in the thinking of the depressed, anxious or addicted
person. We tend to think upsetting things about ourselves
or the world and, crucially, even worse, we start to believe
them with little-to-no supporting evidence. The depressed
and anxious person tends to be negatively biased against
him or herself. The counsellor then went on to inform
me that there are also positive distortions. I said, 'What
ya mean?'

'For instance, if you went around thinking you were
this great perfect person who deserved to get everything
he ever wanted and to be lauded as some sort of a God,
you would be positively distorting reality.'

And I thought to myself, *Are you sure? I kinda felt
that way on Thursday.*

I always thought I had a feelings problem. This recent breakdown was characterised by the return, with a bang, of the uncomfortable feeling, and the best ideas I had to try to get rid of it were to go jogging, cycling and/or meditate, sometimes five or six times a day. And to be fair, as mental as that regime sounds, I did have pockets of time where I seemed to have exorcised the demon and I could get myself back into pretty good form. But I was still running away. The CBT counsellor challenged me to track and record my thoughts when I was feeling both well and not so well. I was stunned to see them written down in front of me.

It turned out that when things were good the inner voice was like a loveable buddy who's always telling ya you're a great lad; my very own hype guy right inside my head. But when I was feeling off I seemed to have an out-and-out prick running the show, speaking to me in a way I couldn't countenance speaking to other people. During that period of feeling unwell there was a day when I probably should (although come to think of it 'should' statements are one of the ten negative distortions) have been working, but as I was quite agitated and low in myself I decided to go for a walk. The interior monologue I documented shocked me: 'Look at the state of ya. Out walking around in circles like a fucking mad person when you should be at work. Christ, you're a pity. Are you ever going to be right? You'd be better off locked up. Or dead.' So much for my theory that I didn't have a thoughts problem.

Everything was starting to become clear now, tangible, with seemingly workable solutions. I won't do CBT justice when I clumsily sum it up as a practical workbook to manage your troubling cognitions. I thought I was somehow going to be taught to not have crazy thoughts, but what's actually on offer are practical measures to hold the thoughts up to scrutiny, shine a light on their lack of supporting evidence and thus empower yourself to choose to believe them or not. I really liked this approach because it seemed to be in line with the one self-help book I ever read that I thought was useful, more than useful. In fact, if I were you I would throw my book in the fire right now, get the 208 bus into town and pick up a copy of it. *Awareness* by Anthony de Mello argues there's nothing wrong with us: states of depression and anxiety will come and go without bothering us as long as we don't try to identify with them and mistakenly see them as who or what we are. CBT seemed to be telling me there's nothing wrong with having wacky or self-destructive thoughts; they're automatic and we all have them. All the problems begin when you take them at face value and believe them.

The day this registered with me, I nearly fell off the chair (I fall off that chair a lot, don't I?) in the counselling session. I got into my car and I drove home feeling like a free man. With the help of the Treeman and an army of other alkies I had found a spiritual solution to my occasional proclivity towards despair. It had worked, it still works and I couldn't do without it. But now through psychotherapy I'd finally confronted my childhood fears, and through CBT I'd acquired practical, scientific techniques to remedy my mad thought processes. I could feel the relief all over my body, a relief I hadn't felt since long before the breakdown. I was finally, truly sorting my shit out.

Do you know when you tell somebody that you're not feeling well – i.e. low mood, anxious etc. – and they come back with 'That's all in your head' and you want to punch them repeatedly in the nose, stomach and groin? Well, it turns out the stupid prick was kinda right. I'm just speaking for myself, of course. I was driving myself insane and miserable with the endless cascade of malicious, masochistic thoughts. CBT helps not only to put the dominant distorted thought on trial, it actually replaces it with one that's more rational, less upsetting. What was once a dip in form that could take days to resolve itself was now taking mere minutes.

The world is fine. It's going about its business just as always. As Anthony de Mello is at pains to point out, the negative thoughts and feelings are not in the world, they're in you. 'Don't ask the world to change – you change first.'

But for all the CBT and psychotherapy in the world, at the end of the day, my friends, I'm an alcoholic – and the best medicine I've ever discovered for alcoholism (other than alcohol) is working with other alkies. And in this, the latest of my many fine meltdowns, I learned some valuable lessons about that too. Much as I'd like to,

I don't seem to be able to coast in alcoholism recovery: if I'm coasting, I'm going backwards. One or two meet-ups with sober alcoholics a month won't cut it for me; I can't keep recovery at a distance. I miss the humility and connectedness with others and I start to feel unique again. Just a unique guy with a unique set of problems and solutions. When the me-ism kicks back in, the thought of doing something for someone else seems like a bit of a chore and very soon I end up back in a prison of my own making.

Around the time I'd started to feel unwell, I had all but stopped meeting other alcoholics and began to prioritise work and some poorly defined idea of success. When I did reach out to other people in recovery again, I felt scared. In my paranoid, low state of mind, I wondered if they would say, 'Oh, here he is, back with his tail between his legs, after going loo laa again.' But of course, they didn't, they never do. They just let you talk or listen or whatever you want to do, identify with you, make you a cup of tea and make you feel part of, again.

As I say, I'm not a big God guy and I'm not a member of any organised religion, but I'm a fully paid-up member of the 'higher power' supporters' club for life. That peace and perfect stillness that comes over you when identifying with another alkie or when in the midst of a particularly deep meditation – well, that started to come back. I suddenly realised what should have been clear all along, that work doesn't matter a toss. OK, it's important to be able to provide for your family but I will never achieve a single thing in my career that'll go any way to filling that void inside myself.

The CBT techniques coupled with finally facing the fear have strengthened my alcoholism recovery, though they could never replace it. For the first time in my life, I've stopped running – figuratively or literally – when the fear comes up, because the fear will still come, the crazy thoughts will still arise. I just don't have to run with them anymore.

Don't get me wrong, exercise is still important for me, but I had to steer away from the 'get up at five o'clock and start running until you hit your head off something' social-media gurus. Brutalising and punishing myself are things I was actually doing in my addiction, so if exercise becomes a hairshirt then it won't work for me. Finding exercise I enjoy was crucial. I learned to swim recently and I'm like a buoyant baby in the pool, splashing about like I just don't care. I also enjoy playing five-a-side soccer and I don't enjoy tracking back, so I won't do it. If you want me on your team you need to be aware that I'm a luxury player. I've a cultured left foot, the odd completely unnecessary trick 'n' flick, the occasional wonder goal, but on a cold night in Churchfield, you will not under any circumstances find me running around after a ball that hasn't been played to my feet.

As I've said, this is not a self-help book and I am not giving you tips on good mental-health practice but here's my absolutely top tip before I leave you. The slow descent into breakdown was characterised by me complaining about everybody and anything that I deemed to be obstructing my path towards greatness. If I'm bitching and moaning I know I've wandered into the zero-sum game mentality; I'm pulling others down to make my scared little self feel better. That's an old idea and it doesn't work anymore. I needed to stop bitching about people and learn to love them again. They annoy me, wear me out and disappoint me daily but by God, I bloody love people and I can't live without the magic of connecting with them, understanding them, laughing with them, sharing their pain and their madness. I can't make it on my own. You are almost certainly a person, reader, and I have just told you that I love you. Would it kill you to say it back?

Chapter Twelve

Nice Things to Be at When You're Not Demented

When I came into recovery in 2015 – with my hands in the air, knowing the jig was finally up, I really just had one goal, one desire: I wanted not to take my own life. I didn't want to leave my daughter without a father. I had surmised that wanting anything more, like a bit of happiness or contentment, was pushing my luck. I still had a very all-or-nothing outlook on life: my drinking life had been debauched and sinful, and now that I found myself in recovery and wanted to be good, my job was to grin and bear it.

Recovery from addiction was still somewhat punitive in my mind and I'd have sat in misery as long as I managed to stay alive and off the booze. I'd have settled for that. I'd have been grateful. I was so tired of battling my own head, of perennially hurting other people and letting them down, of dizzying myself with a merry-go-round of drinking, trying to manage, trying to stop, trying to go back on it, *ad nauseam*. I reckon this is pretty normal for someone in recovery. My heart breaks with empathy for the young person trying to embrace a drink- and drug-free life when all their mates are still at it.

The sober alcoholics I met early on were laughing and full of gratitude. There was a real buzz of vitality and hope and togetherness. I remember sitting there thinking, *This is nice but it's obviously a performance for my benefit, a sham.* Don't get me wrong – I saw it as a well-meaning sham; a group consensus that they would paint smiles on their faces and make the very best of this torturous, unthinkable half-life we'd been consigned to for the sake of the new, poor, suffering soul who had joined them. I really did feel that it was impossible to be happy, laughing, having fun and be 'off the drink', let alone 'sober', whatever that meant.

And, of course, initial attempts to be a non-drinker in a drinkers' society can be nightmarish. You suddenly realise what a masterful aid to even basic social inter- actions and obstacles alcohol is. I remember being in a nightclub early on in recovery, attempting to dance, to look cool and blend in at an event mostly populated by people off their trolleys. I came face to face with a stark, ugly truth: I can't dance. I dance like a big, weird-looking doll being puppeteered by a peevish child. Jerky, robotic, un-rhythmic movements, a seriously shook look on my face and a furious battle of wills going on between my head and my feet. To this day, there's probably noth- ing on earth that torments me and makes my blood go as cold as being lobbied to dance at some gathering or other. There, on the dance floor, I suddenly realised why I'd been taking amphetamines for all those years: to avoid ever having to glance down and soberly watch my body trying in vain to keep a beat. And of course, in your head, everyone is looking at you. A buddy in recovery calls it the star-attraction mentality. They're all looking at me now. They're all thinking, *Why isn't he drinking? What's wrong with him? What a freak.* Whereas, in actual fact, nobody gives a fuck about ya (in a generally good way!); they're mostly trying to buy pills in the toilet or to console their friend who's roaring crying about her ex.

The greater public reinforces this fear of dry pubbing/clubbing. I have often found myself in conversations with people who either wonder or downright demand to know what fun I could possibly be having in a pub, club or party without alcohol. I'm not judging them for a minute, that's exactly how I felt when I was forced to stop. But then a few years later, on a night out during Cork's Midsummer Festival, I found myself at a brilliant play in the honeymoon suite in the Clayton Hotel, then going to a pub and a club afterwards and ending up back in the suite for an after-party. I left at about five o'clock in the morning and, strolling home, I realised that for maybe the first time in my life, I hadn't thought about the fact that I wasn't drinking on a night out. Normally it would be at the forefront of my mind, but instead, I'd been chatting to interesting people, immersed in a great show, free from my head. I felt no lack, no insecurity. I'd had a great night not just booze-free but booze-obsession free. And I realised that, for me at least, the superpower that is alcohol is only really super and vital when you feel ill at ease. I wonder how many of us are getting blind drunk because it takes away that dreadful feeling of insecurity when you first walk into the pub or party?

Since then, I've had many more fun evenings watching and performing comedy, music and theatre than I've had drinking. Contrary to popular belief, we alcoholics are not longingly casting glimpses at your pints, resisting the urge to whip them out of your hands and throw them all over our heads and mouths and chins and necks. When you start to feel at ease with yourself, getting speechlessly drunk starts to lose its appeal. Again, I'm not judging anyone. If I weren't an anxious alcoholic myself, who'd suffered the almost fatal consequences of bouts of drinking, I'd absolutely still be at it.

To the people who can go out, have a few drinks, come home, go to bed, go to work without feeling like they'd like to end their life – we salute you, we're fascinated by you and we wish you well. Our cautionary tales don't apply to you. I'm just hoping to offer a ray of light to the alcoholic or potential alcoholic who may realise that they're running out of road and yet feels like a lifetime in recovery is effectively a death sentence. If you're open and honest and you're willing to put the work in, life is just about to start, not end. You won't need to be drunk anymore to cope with the burden of being you. You'll wish your drunk buddies well but you'll no longer feel compelled to join them. You won't be smug or judgemental; you'll neither be better nor worse than your fellows. You'll just feel alright. You'll reach an unimaginable summit in an Irish context: having booze-free fun. Imagine that.

When I was drinking, sitting on bar stools or on couches in gaffs, looking out the window at the birds, resentfully listening to them sing their morning reper-toire, daydreaming about the life I could be living, my core desires were modest. Apart from wanting to never treat people like shit again, there were always three things I wanted for myself if I were to ever get sober: learn to drive, learn to swim and go back and relearn the Irish language. Each of these had symbolic impor-tance to me – they were things I said I would do and never did throughout my drinking life and so became synonymous with the inertia, lack of resolve and bro-ken promises of active addiction. After about a year in recovery, I'd had some motoring guidance from Claire and had learned the basics in a little yellow Mini named Lily. Claire loved her, it seemed to me, more than life itself. How I was allowed anywhere near her is surely another testament to her love and unfounded belief in my abilities.

Trying to learn to drive in a yellow Mini as a con-fused, newly sober addict in his thirties was as challeng-ing as it sounds. I cut out on the College Road one night and this obnoxious lad in a Beemer began beeping the shit out of me from behind. I felt sure he was only doing it because he thought there was a young girl in the car ahead of him, and I felt I owed it to young learner girls everywhere to jump out of the car, pull this man out his driver's window and wreak hell on his self-absorbed ass. Thankfully, Claire pulled me back into the car.

Driving around in the yellow Mini gave me a new lease of life. I felt I was undoing some of the wrongs whenever I'd pick my daughter up from school or bring her to violin lessons. I should have been driving years ago. I'd wanted to. I felt embarrassed every time I'd find myself walking the streets with Caoimhe in the pouring rain after missing the bus. But my drinking was always just that bit more important; driving was expensive and limited my lifestyle. So I obeyed my thirst. But now, here I was, obeying my values.

I also felt proud of myself for overcoming the fear of driving itself, with or without an alcoholic head. When I was working in the RTÉ kids' show years earlier, I'd bought a Honda 50 motorbike for 400 quid because I thought I'd look cool on it. I took it out once, driving really, really slowly down the road and onto a nearby field. I went out over the handlebars twice, walked it home and sold it a few days later for 400 quid. Cash back! When that is your only driving experience, driving around the city in a yellow Mini with an encouraging buddy in the passenger seat, regularly cutting out or not, is a massive achievement.

Eventually my friend's dad L, the guy who had thrown the arms around me when I'd stood in his hallway, quite mad, the day my own father passed away, sorted me out with an old-but-plucky Renault Clio. And Claire handed me over to the care of Bishopstown's most renowned driving instructor. He had his hands full and literally retired straight after completing the last lesson with me. The night we finished up, I asked him how he felt about my chances of passing the test. He said, 'You might as well do it anyway, boy, there's no harm in chancing it.' *I beg to differ*, I thought, *there's plenty of potential harm*.

To regular folk, it's hard to describe how important bucket lists are for those of us in recovery from addiction. It's not about ticking a box; it's about proving to yourself that you are not the write-off you once believed you were. It's about defying the odds by not merely surviving but thriving with all the things you could only fantasise about being able to do when you were on the sidelines of life in your cups. It feels as if you're finally walking through the doors of *Stars in their Eyes*. 'Tonight, Matthew, I'm going to be a responsible human being who now participates in life in a somewhat normal manner!'

The day of the test, I knew my abilities weren't quite up to scratch but I was still really proud of myself for getting this far with the driving dream. Luck was on my side as the fella who sat into my little car was a big, burly, lovable-grandfather type. A young lad also waiting in the car park looked enviously at me as the Werther's Original grandad stooped and flopped into my micro-machine. We drove around the Sarsfield Road roundabout and wound up in Togher, where he taught me how to reverse around a corner and get the condensation off my side windows. On paper, effectively receiving a lesson from your examiner wouldn't be a good omen, but the old childhood ego kicked back in and I started to tell myself that it had gone well, that I'd already passed and these were bonus tweaks from one lovable rogue to another.

Almost unbelievably, my positively distorted thoughts were correct, or he felt sorry for me, or both. He passed me, gave me a little tap on the shoulder and said, 'You're not bad at all.' Perfect. I left the centre and met herself back at the car. I'm not ashamed to tell you we both cried, me with pride and her with disbelief. The lad walking through the rain with his little girl had finally put on his big-boy pants.

There were many mishaps and false dawns along the swimming journey, too. My first teacher was an extremely critical Englishwoman who gave me notes even under the water. I naturally couldn't hear what she was saying but her face looked really cross, and I then I got cross and started thinking, this is what happens now when you reach out to the English and try to build bridges, they attempt to drown you in the local leisure centre. It is only in the last year that a girl about my daughter's age, wise beyond her years, has taken me from a lad splashing around like a cat to what some people are saying is Cork South Central's answer to Michelle Smith de Brun. Front crawl, backstroke, breaststroke, lying-on-your-back-looking-at-the-ceiling stroke: you name it, I stroke it.

When I was younger, I couldn't do anything for myself. I didn't even know what to order in a restaurant. My first trip to Edinburgh I got through on a diet of Tennent's, Ecstasy tablets and Centrum vitamins. I could never pay a bill, book a holiday or meet with authority figures of any description. Towards the end of my drinking, I was actually falling off my bicycle I was so rattled. Now, I'm driving and swimming. I could get up some day now if I wanted to and drive to the beach and go on away in, swimming. Imagine that.

I've also started doing courses with Gaelchultúr. A lovely woman up the country coaxed me into doing my first stand-up comedy gig *as Gaeilge* (in Irish) for Lá Fhéile Pádraig in Naas recently and from what people tell me, I may have single-handedly started a renaissance of the language. I don't know. I'm just a man. I'm nowhere near *liofa* (fluent) but, like the swimming and the driving, I kind of know that after many false starts, this is my time. I might just be weeks away from driving to the beach *and* shouting expletives *as Gaeilge* when I first dive into the water.

Another one of my new-life projects is politics. One of the many tough sides to being a perennially lying and spoofing alcoholic is that your friends lose respect for you. They stop thinking of you as a serious person. For years, I'd been blabbering on about half-baked notions of solidarity, the right to protest and a smorgasbord of other leftist mantras. I remember going on about Palestine one time in an early-morning house. A buddy interrupted me: 'There's a rally for Palestine in town today, are you saying a few words at it?' The whole table started laughing. I was a spoofer. Slowly but surely, with the drink put down and the head getting back in range, I started to walk the walk. I began to go to the marches, be they for Palestine, Scottish and Welsh independence movements, or causes at home. I started doing some fundraising and just generally playing my little part through the comedy.

Since school, I've been obsessed with nations and flags, with history and politics. My copybooks used to be full of national flags and you'd be doing well to beat me in the capital-cities round of a quiz. I always felt a great affinity with the north of Ireland, for some reason. I grew up in a fairly apolitical house. My mother was off in her own world and my dad was more concerned with how to make ends meet than what was going on in the North, depicted as it was by southern media as a bit of a basket case that had nothing to do with us. The really strong impression I got as a kid, from RTÉ and the newspapers, was that republicans were to blame for all the violence and misery. They had maliciously commandeered our flag and shamed our good name.

I remember as a twelve- or thirteen-year-old reading weekly articles in the *Independent,* vilifying John Hume for having the audacity to even speak to republicans. Even at that age, I just kind of knew that Hume was an unlikely villain. He would, of course, go on to be one of the more popular recipients of the Nobel Peace prize. If our media's portrayal of Hume was so embarrassingly inaccurate, what other parts of the northern picture were missing? From doing my own reading, I learned that, like every conflict since time began, this one was entirely more complicated and contextual than the *Independent* would have us believe. I learned more about republican violence but also about loyalist paramilitaries and their long history of collusion with the British state. I learned about the pogroms and second-class citizenship of northern nationalists, from the foundation of Northern Ireland until the outbreak of the Troubles in 1969, and I learned that the South did little but watch on, shrugging its shoulders as the drawbridge was pulled up and Irish citizens became partitioned in an apartheid state – at least, this is my interpretation. I'm aware that I'm on the verge of delivering an unwanted TED Talk here, guys. I assure you I'm just about to stop.

I have no desire to celebrate the actions or legacy of any military group or absolve any actors of responsibility. And needless to say, I'm no expert. I'm just an ex-drunk with a library card. What I'm saying is that the idea that one group is exclusively responsible, and that the South is somehow detached from any role in the descent into the Troubles, seemed unhelpful and fantastical to me. Rather than championing a side, it was really southern hypocrisy which lit a flame under my political arse.

On leaving school, I thought about studying up north. I thought about getting involved in politics, or even just bloody visiting the place. These are all wonderful ideas until you go drinking for four days, wake up in a house you don't recognise, can't find your shoes and need to prepare yourself for a week of recriminations, self-loathing and soul-searching. I was not a functional drunk: most of the time I was living or drinking, and rarely the two would meet. Addiction robs you of your ability to act in accordance with your convictions and values. There's no time for anything else when the self-centredness of Gatmania takes over.

After a few years of being on the straight and narrow, I've travelled all over the North, gained a lot more understanding than I ever got from books and documentaries, and made many new friends: nationalists, unionists and neither. I've been lucky enough to produce comedy work on my specialised subject also, which has travelled all around the world, but that's not really what warms the cockles of my heart. It's when new friends in Derry or Belfast occasionally thank me for playing some small part in getting the South to, in their view, face up to its historical amnesia about the North. That means a lot to me. That stuff alerts me to the fact that I'm living a life beyond my wildest dreams.

I need to feel useful. I felt useless for too long. If I went into specifics about the lovely things I've done for people since I've got sober I'd bore the poop out of ya and I'd be falling into the old ego trap again. But suffice to say, my altruistic acts are many, beautiful and if you'd like more information about them, I've attached my email address at the end of this frankly superb book.

I remember leaving a gaff on the Lower Glanmire Road one morning. I'd been sober for a few months but I'd broken out again. I walked down by the bus station – more like scurried actually, like a little drowned rat, eyes darting around, scanning for someone who might know me so I could look the other way. I watched people pulling up shutters or pounding the pavements in high heels and business shoes, taking on the new day whether they wanted to or not, going to work, earning money for themselves and their families, contributing. I was an outsider to all this. I asked myself, What I was bringing to the table? I had something to offer but I didn't know how to conjure it up and present it. I felt useless. And I think that useless is only one rung of the ladder above hopeless.

One of the joys of being in recovery is the slow and steady way in which usefulness comes back into your life. It can begin with something as simple as washing up the cups after a bunch of alcoholics meet up and can extend all the way to feeling so good and comfortable in yourself that you can put out your hand and play a small part in helping someone else getting back on their feet. I have the absolute privilege these days of meeting up with young alcoholics who are starting their own journey of self-acceptance, accountability and personal growth. I'm yet to experience anything as beautiful as being a transmitter of a message of recovery, a cheerleader for someone else in their healing journey and not being up in my own head, spoiling it with thoughts of, *Aren't I a great lad?* I'm not a bad lad, I'm no better or worse than any other lad, but I'm very grateful to be a useful lad.

Epilogue

I'll Finish on This

So here I am backstage at the Everyman Theatre, about to head out to MC this gorgeous night of song and music and new-Irish community Christmas spirit. The Everyman has made a brave choice in selecting me as MC and I commend them for it. I'm not the most seamless or efficient master of ceremonies in the business and on this particular evening, I only remember to introduce myself just before the last performance. I also forget to do the fire announcement. They were the only two things written on the sheet of paper they'd handed me at the start.

I'm the kind of performer who often relies on the kindness and understanding of the audience, and you better believe that tonight is one of those evenings. Claire, her mother and a host of other family and friends are in the audience giving me vocal, not always complimentary, feedback on how I'm doing throughout the evening. I sing a song myself, a Nat King Cole number and dedicate it to herself. I tell the Everyman, and I suppose I'm now telling you, that we are expecting our first child together. I'm going to be a dad again. I have such a great relationship with Caoimhe today (thanks to recovery) but it is some buzz to be starting that journey again, sober. To think about how many moments I'm going to experience that I must have missed before. Bumpín, or at least this particular Bumpín, couldn't have existed had I fallen through the cracks of life and my own thinking as I nearly did so many times. But I survived. I found a solution. The whole of the Everyman claps and cheers for the unborn new buddy. Getting a rapturous response from the crowd before he/she is even born: classic Hickey.

And looking out at the audience I suddenly think of the perfect place for my inner child to hang out. I think Bubbsie would approve. I was supposed to bring him somewhere where he'd feel safe and have a laugh. This place is perfect. Standing up here on the Everyman stage, cracking (dad) jokes and sharing our news about the imminent arrival of a new kid on the block, I put my inner child sitting up on the balcony, in the front row, gazing down on the stage in awe. He is happy out, clapping and laughing. And if he feels a bit scared, he doesn't have to panic anymore, it's grand. I reassure him. 'It's OK, kid, I have ya.'

Acknowledgements

First and foremost, I wish to thank the one and only Deirdre Nolan (Eriu/Bonnier) for saying out loud what my positive cognitive distortions have been whispering to me all my life: there's a book in you, boy! Thank you for your dedication and friendship. To my crack team of editors, Liz Marvin, Leonie Lock and Djinn von Noorden, led by the sensational Alison Walsh. You turned a hot mess into what some people* are saying is the best book of all time. *(These people may not be real.)

To the invisible army of recovering alcoholics (led by the Treeman) who save my skin every day: I'll never be able to convey how grateful I am to you for helping me live to tell my tale.

My non-alcoholic buddies, you know who are.

My family. My big brothers. My sister who's been my biggest fan, counsellor and sister-in-arms since I used to catch her by the hand and follow her everywhere she went, even into her school to watch Christmas movies!

And Claire. Not just for her help with this book but for her help with this life. You make everything brighter and better.

And blessed as I am amongst women, I'd lastly like to thank my daughter(s), Caoimhe and the new kid on the block, Sadhbh. Thank you for the love you put in my heart. You're quite simply the best things that ever happened to me.